WORLD BANK STAFF WORKING PAPERS
Number 652

Recent Chinese Economic Reforms

Studies of Two Industrial Enterprises

William Byrd
Gene Tidrick
Chen Jiyuan
Xu Lu
Tang Zongkun
Chen Lantong

The World Bank
Washington, D.C., U.S.A.

Manufactured in the United States of America
First printing September 1984

This is a working document published informally by the World Bank. To present the results of research with the least possible delay, the typescript has not been prepared in accordance with the procedures appropriate to formal printed texts, and the World Bank accepts no responsibility for errors. The publication is supplied at a token charge to defray part of the cost of manufacture and distribution.

The views and interpretations in this document are those of the author(s) and should not be attributed to the World Bank, to its affiliated organizations, or to any individual acting on their behalf. Any maps used have been prepared solely for the convenience of the readers; the denominations used and the boundaries shown do not imply, on the part of the World Bank and its affiliates, any judgment on the legal status of any territory or any endorsement or acceptance of such boundaries.

The full range of World Bank publications, both free and for sale, is described in the *Catalog of Publications;* the continuing research program is outlined in *Abstracts of Current Studies.* Both booklets are updated annually; the most recent edition of each is available without charge from the Publications Sales Unit, Department T, The World Bank, 1818 H Street, N.W., Washington, D.C. 20433, U.S.A., or from the European Office of the Bank, 66 avenue d'Iéna, 75116 Paris, France.

William Byrd is an economist and Gene Tidrick a senior economist in the China Programs Division of the World Bank. Chen Jiyuan and Tang Zongkun are associate researchers and Chen Lantong an engineer in the Institute of Economics of the Chinese Academy of Social Sciences. Xu Lu is a senior economist and member of the Editorial Committee of *Jingji Yanjiu* [Economic Research].

Library of Congress Cataloging in Publication Data

Main entry under title:

Recent Chinese economic reforms.

(World Bank staff working papers ; no. 652)
1. Industry and state--China--Case studies.
2. Industrial management--China--Case studies. I. Byrd, William, 1952- . II. Series.
HD3616.C63R43 1984 338.951 84-19513
ISBN 0-8213-0412-7

Abstract

This paper consists of two studies of Chinese industrial enterprises and their response to national policies of adjustment and reform in recent years. "Adjustment and Reform in the Chongqing Clock and Watch Company" analyzes the effect of economic reforms and adjustment policies on a consumer durables producer in 1980-82. This enterprise has often been cited as an advanced enterprise in reforms; it has been given control over a number of subordinate firms, responsibility for profit and loss, autonomy in the use of funds and in investment decisions, and the right to market its products directly.

The incentives created by reforms are analyzed in the light of the enterprise's objective function, with particular attention to the interaction between changes in incentives and changes in market conditions. The main conclusions are that the dominant influence on the enterprise has been the market, external controls have been weak and manipulable, labor allocation remains the most unreformed part of the system, and use of bank loans to finance investment has loosened rather than strengthened financial discipline. Finally, reforms achieved their aims only after the "seller's market" for the enterprise's output had been transformed into a "buyer's market."

"Management Reforms in the Qingdao Forging Machinery Plant" analyzes the effect of adjustment and reform policies on a medium-sized machinery producer. This factory was given financial incentives and made responsible for sales at the same time that demand for its products fell sharply as a result of a reduction in national investment and heavy industry output. In this crisis the enterprise responded by initiating an economic responsibility system of management, making an intensive sales effort, drastically changing its product mix, and attempting to improve the quality of and diversify its products. It is argued that conflicting directives from overlapping supervisory agencies, a largely unreformed labor and wage system, and price controls which hold down profit margins have hurt the plant's performance despite considerable improvements resulting from the reforms that have been implemented.

Abrégé

Le présent exposé traite de deux entreprises industrielles chinoises et de la manière dont elles ont réagi aux politiques nationales d'ajustement et de réforme qui ont été mises en oeuvre ces dernières années. La section intitulée "Ajustement et réforme dans l'entreprise d'horlogerie de Chongqing" examine l'effet des réformes économiques et des politiques d'ajustement des années 1980 à 1982 sur un producteur de biens de consommation durables. Souvent citée en exemple comme étant parmi les plus avancées dans l'application des réformes, cette entreprise a reçu la charge d'un certain nombre de sociétés moins importantes; elle est devenue responsable de ses profits et pertes, autonome en matière d'investissement et d'utilisation des fonds et libre de commercialiser directement ses produits.

Les mesures d'incitation mises en place dans le cadre des réformes sont analysées en fonction de la vocation objective de l'entreprise; l'accent est mis en particulier sur les interactions entre ces encouragements et le marché. Il ressort de cette étude que c'est le marché qui a exercé l'influence la plus marquante sur l'entreprise, que le contrôle extérieur a été faible et aisément manipulé, que l'affectation de la main-d'oeuvre reste le facteur qui a été le moins réformé et que le recours à l'emprunt bancaire pour financer les investissements a provoqué un relâchement de la discipline financière au lieu de la renforcer. Enfin, les réformes n'ont atteint leur but qu'après que les marchés des produits de l'entreprise, jusque-là favorables au vendeur, se furent transformés en marchés favorisant l'acheteur.

La section intitulée "Réformes de gestion dans l'usine de machines de forage de Qingdao" analyse les répercussions des mesures d'ajustement et des réformes sur un producteur moyen de machines. Cette usine s'est vue accorder des incitations financières et confier la responsabilité des ventes à une époque où la demande de ses produits avait brutalement chuté, à la suite de la réduction des investissements nationaux et de la baisse de production des industries lourdes. L'entreprise a réagi à cette crise en mettant en place un système de gestion fondé sur la responsabilité économique, en déployant un effort intensif de vente, en changeant radicalement sa gamme de produits et en s'efforçant de diversifier sa production et d'en améliorer la qualité. Il est démontré que, malgré les améliorations considérables qu'ont apportées les réformes, les résultats de l'entreprise ont été affectés par trois facteurs : les organismes de tutelle, dont les domaines de compétence se recoupent, ont publié des directives contradictoires, les dispositions en matière de main-d'oeuvre et de salaires sont restées pratiquement inchangées et les marges bénéficiaires ont souffert du contrôle des prix.

Extracto

El presente documento consta de dos estudios sobre empresas industriales de China y sus reacciones ante las políticas nacionales de ajuste y reforma de años recientes. El primero, titulado "Ajuste y reforma en la Compañía de Relojes de Chongqing", analiza los efectos de las reformas económicas y las políticas de ajuste sobre un productor de bienes de consumo duraderos en 1980-82. A menudo se ha citado a esta empresa como una empresa avanzada en materia de reformas; se le ha dado el control de cierto número de firmas subordinadas, responsabilidades en materia de pérdidas y ganancias, autonomía para la utilización de fondos y en decisiones sobre inversión, y el derecho a comercializar directamente sus productos.

Los incentivos creados por las reformas se analizan a la luz de la función objetiva de la empresa prestando especial atención a la acción mutua entre las modificaciones en los incentivos y los cambios en las condiciones del mercado. Las conclusiones principales son de que la influencia predominante en la empresa ha sido el mercado, los controles externos han sido débiles y susceptibles de manipulación, la asignación de la mano de obra sigue siendo la parte menos reformada del sistema y el empleo de los préstamos bancarios para financiar la inversión ha relajado, en lugar de fortalecer, la disciplina financiera. Por último, las reformas lograron sus objetivos solamente después que el "mercado de vendedores" para los productos de la empresa se hubo transformado en "mercado de compradores".

El segundo estudio, "Reformas administrativas en la Planta de Maquinaria para Forjado de Qingdao", analiza los efectos de las políticas de ajuste y reforma sobre un productor de maquinaria de tamaño mediano. Esta fábrica recibió incentivos financieros y se le asignó responsabilidad en cuanto a las ventas en momentos en que la demanda de sus productos decaía considerablemente a consecuencia de una reducción en las inversiones nacionales y la producción de la industria pesada. Frente a esta crisis la empresa respondió implantando un sistema de gestión de responsabilidad económica, emprendiendo una intensa campaña de ventas, modificando drásticamente su gama de productos y procurando mejorar la calidad y diversificar su producción. Se arguye en el estudio que las normas en conflicto expedidas por organismos de supervisión que se superponen unos a otros, un régimen laboral y de salarios en general no reformado y los controles de precios que limitan los márgenes de utilidad han perjudicado el buen desempeño de la planta a pesar de mejoras considerables a consecuencia de las reformas que se han implantado.

Acknowledgements

These two reports are the first products of a collaborative research project between the Institute of Economics of the Chinese Academy of Social Sciences (CASS) and the World Bank. One component of the research project is a study of enterprise guidance, which is defined broadly to include internal management issues, relations among enterprises, and relations between them and government authorities. The main source of information for the project will be in-depth interviews in 20 enterprises and organizations. The present reports are based upon the first two such interviews, conducted jointly by researchers from CASS and the World Bank. The conclusions presented are tentative. Analysis based on information from all 20 enterprises will be published at a later date. The principal researchers on the CASS team were Chen Jiyuan (team leader), Xu Lu, Tang Zongkun and Chen Lantong. Principal researchers on the World Bank team were Gene Tidrick (team leader), William Byrd, David Granick (consultant), and Josephine Woo. The overall research is supervised by Dong Fureng, Deputy Director of the Institute of Economics, and Greg Ingram and Edwin Lim of the World Bank.

The authors wish to thank the Chongqing Clock and Watch Company, the Qingdao Forging Machinery Plant, and the economic departments of Chongqing and Qingdao municipalities and Jiaoxian County. Without their cooperation these reports could not have been written. The authors of each report benefited from comments made during discussions between the two teams. However, the authors of each report remain solely responsible for the views and interpretations expressed.

Table of Contents

Summary

Since 1978, numerous economic policy changes have occurred in China as part of the Government's new strategy of adjustment and reform. Adjustment has meant changing the economic structure by increasing consumption at the expense of investment and emphasizing agriculture and light (consumer) industry rather than heavy industry. The main thrust of reform has been to decentralize economic decision-making and to rely more on the market to provide incentives and guide decisions. Reforms have been most far-reaching in agriculture, but in industry, too, China has moved away from its traditional central planning system.

These two papers analyze the effect of adjustment and reform on two enterprises during 1980-82. Reforms were most extensive for the Chongqing Clock and Watch Company (CCWC), but the Qingdao Forging Machinery Plant (QFMP) was also affected by reforms giving it the right to retain a share of profits and the responsibility for sales as well as production. A more important difference between the two enterprises was the contrast in market conditions. Like most producers of consumer durables, CCWC produced a highly profitable product enjoying considerable pent-up demand. QFMP faced a sharp reduction in demand for its somewhat outmoded, low profit margin products. However, market conditions for clocks and watches quickly changed and the interesting aspect of CCWC's experience is not how it took advantage of expansion opportunities but rather how it, like QFMP, responded to the change from a seller's to a buyer's market and how reforms shaped its response.

From 1980, CCWC participated in several reforms of a very advanced type: it gained responsibility for sales, changed its organizational form into that of a corporation in charge of several subordinate factories, formed numerous joint ventures and associations with other enterprises, and converted from a system of handing over profits to one of taxation, with responsibility for profits and losses as well as considerable autonomy in the use of its funds. CCWC took advantage of initial excess demand and its increased autonomy to expand production rapidly through mergers and investments financed by retained profits and bank loans. Saturation of the clock market and a centrally-imposed limit on watch production created a difficult situation, in which CCWC responded by trying to alter the rules governing its decisions, by aggressively promoting sales through disguised price reductions and other methods, and by improving product quality and variety. The company has only recently begun to search for ways to reduce costs of production.

In both its expansion and problem-solving phases, CCWC behaved as predicted by economic theory for an enterprise facing price controls under changing market conditions. However, CCWC was not trying to maximize profits, average value added per worker, managerial income or any of the other objective functions normally assumed in anlyzing capitalist or other socialist economies. The objective of Chinese enterprises appears to be to maximize total family income and benefits of workers. Under the incentives and constraints operating at CCWC, this led to behavior best modelled by positing a maximand of total net product. This means that CCWC was more expansionist than a profit-maximizing or conventional labor-managed enterprise would be. The reformed incentive system under which CCWC operated was largely neutral with respect to factor use, but the complicated system of capital taxes and deductions made borrowing more attractive than self-financed investment.

Reforms also gave the Qingdao Forging Machinery Plant the right to retain some profits and to borrow from banks, as well as responsibility for sales and for profit and loss. However, QFMP retained a smaller share of profits than CCWC, did not have the authority of a corporation and, most importantly, almost immediately faced a sharp contraction in demand for its products due to the cutback in activity of heavy industry. From the outset, therefore, QFMP faced a buyer's market. Moreover, it received conflicting directives from overlapping supervisory agencies and faced considerably more problems in obtaining raw materials than did CCWC.

QFMP responded to these problems by initiating an internal economic responsibility system of management, an intensive sales effort, and a shift in product mix in response to the market, and by attempting to improve and diversify its products. After an initial decline in output and profits, these efforts have succeeded in improving the plant's performance. However, QFMP is still hampered by "multi-headed" leadership, a largely unreformed labor and wage system, and a low profit margin on most products.

The paper by Byrd and Tidrick draws several conclusions which are applicable to both enterprises. First, the dominant influence on both firms has been the market, not directive plans. Second, financial incentives and planning systems are both weak and manipulable at the enterprise level. Third, the unreformed labor allocation system distorts enterprise decisions. Fourth, increased use of investment financing through bank loans are generally loosened rather than strengthened financial discipline. Finally, the program of adjustment and Reform has tended to achieve its avowed aim of promoting intensive rather than extensive growth, but only after seller's market conditions have been eliminated.

ADJUSTMENT AND REFORM IN THE CHONGQING CLOCK AND WATCH COMPANY

William Byrd and Gene Tidrick

ADJUSTMENT AND REFORM IN THE CHONGQING CLOCK AND WATCH COMPANY

Table of Contents

TABLES

FIGURES

1. INTRODUCTION

The Relevance of CCWC as a Case Study

1.01 The recent history of the Chongqing Clock and Watch Company (CCWC) provides an interesting case study of Chinese adjustment and reform policies.[1/] As a producer of consumer durable goods, CCWC benefitted from policies favoring light industry and the growth of consumption. On the demand side, rapidly growing consumer incomes added to existing unsatisfied demand for watches. On the supply side, CCWC was encouraged to expand production and was given the means to do so through a variety of reforms discussed below. CCWC may be a fairly typical example of how China was able to achieve such impressive growth of consumer durables production during the past several years.[2/]

1.02 CCWC's experience is also typical in another respect. Consumer durables industries all over the world are vulnerable to market saturation and overexpansion. A classic argument for central planning is that it can prevent business cycles and overinvestment by coordinating production and investment decisions. In consumer durables industries the Chinese authorities faced a dilemma. They felt the need to decentralize decisionmaking in order to improve incentives to expand production and upgrade quality, but decentralization, especially for inexperienced enterprises in a highly profitable industry, carried the risk of overexpansion and market saturation. In fact, the clock market did become saturated by the end of 1981, competition sharpened in the watch market, and the planning authorities intervened to slow the growth of watch production. CCWC thus presents an example of how an enterprise responds to increased autonomy and how the planning authorities sought to give effect to the slogan "planned economy as primary and market regulation as auxiliary". The interesting aspect of CCWC's experience is not how it took advantage of expansion opportunities but rather how it has responded to problems which have arisen and how the reforms have shaped the company's response. This experience is highly relevant because the problems faced by CCWC in marketing its products are typical of many consumer durables industries in China and similar to the problems machinery producers have been facing since even earlier.

1/ In late 1978, the Chinese Government launched a new economic strategy of adjustment and reform. This emphasized development of agriculture and light industry, raised urban wages and agricultural procurement prices, and introduced several experiments with decentralized decisionmaking and greater use of markets to improve producer incentives. For a detailed description, see World Bank, China: Socialist Economic Development, (Washington, 1983), Volume I, pp. 146-71.

2/ From 1978 to 1982 output of light industry grew by 56.6% compared to only 14.4% for heavy industry. Within light industry, the growth of consumer durables production was particularly rapid, ranging from 164% for sewing machines to 1,044% for televisions.

1.03 Perhaps the chief interest of CCWC rests in its position as a reformed enterprise. It is located in Sichuan Province, which has been in the forefront of the reform movement, and it has participated in several reforms of a very advanced type. Most notably, CCWC has been made responsible for sales, has been changed into a corporation in charge of several subordinate factories, has formed numerous joint ventures and associations with other enterprises, and has converted from a system of handing over profits to one of taxation, with supposedly full responsibility for profits and losses as well as considerable autonomy in the use of its funds.

1.04 CCWC has been held up as a model of reform on several fronts.[3/] It was one of only 456 enterprises nationwide to have participated in various experiments substituting taxes for profit delivery,[4/] and its example undoubtedly influenced the decision to introduce a national program of limited conversion to taxation. In March 1983, Finance Minister Wang Bingqian led a team which investigated experiments and drew up plans for conversion to a taxation system in Chongqing.[5/] CCWC was one of the enterprises visited. Moreover, unlike experiments in many other enterprises, the reforms in CCWC have remained fairly stable. The tax rate was fixed for three years from January 1, 1980, and most other aspects have also been stable for three years. Although it is difficult to disentangle the impact of adjustment policies and special circumstances from the effects of reforms, this is a sufficiently long period of stability to make an initial attempt to analyze the impact of reforms on the company's behavior.

1.05 In brief, CCWC is a typical beneficiary of national adjustment policies but atypical of Chinese enterprises in the advanced degree of its reforms. Thus its experience provides an interesting microeconomic study of the impact of Chinese adjustment and reform policies and the attempt to shift from extensive to intensive industrial development.

3/ See, for example, "Chongqing Clock and Watch Company Develops Joint Operation and Promotes Specialized Cooperation," in State Economic Commission, Selections on Industrial Management, 1981, (Beijing: Renmin Chubanshe, 1981) and Gu Zongzhan, "Problems Concerning the Practice of Making State-Operated Enterprises Responsible for their own Profits and Losses," Economic Management, 1980(12). For more recent and detailed studies of CCWC see: Yu Zuyao, "Investigation of the Chongqing Clock and Watch Company's Experiment of Substituting Tax Payments for Profit Remittances," Finance and Trade Economics, 1983(6), pp. 51-54; and Xu Lu, "The Economic Responsibility System in Industry: An Investigation of the Chongqing Clock and Watch Company," Economic Investigations, No. 1 (October 1983), pp. 37-40.

4/ This is the figure given in "Finance Official Answers Questions on New Taxation System," Xinhua News Agency, April 27, 1983, as reported in BBC, FE/7327/C/4, May 7, 1983.

5/ "Chongqing State-Owned Industrial Enterprises Converted from Profit Remittance to Taxation from May 1," People's Daily, May 4, 1983, p.2.

The Chinese Clock and Watch Industry

1.06 China began producing clocks in 1915 and watches in 1955.[6/] In 1981 China produced 27.7 million clocks and 28.7 million watches and was the fifth largest producer of watches in the world. About 35% of clock production and nearly 10% of watch output in that year was exported.[7/] There are more than 100 factories producing clocks, watches, and basic parts or semi-finished materials; only six provinces do not produce at least some watches. However, the Shanghai Clock and Watch Company dominates the industry. It produced 9.3 million watches in 1981, one third of the national total, and the largest Shanghai factory alone produced nearly 5 million watches.[8/]

1.07 Watch production grew rapidly from a very small base in the 1960s (Table 1.1). The growth rate fell below 20% in the early 1970s but then accelerated again after 1976, despite the much larger base of production. Amid growing signs of possible overexpansion of consumer durables production capacity, a national conference was called in September 1981 to draw up a production plan for major light industry products through 1985. The 1985 national target for watch production was set at 45 million, thus limiting the

---

6/ Most of the following general information on the Chinese industry is from Ministry of Light Industry, "China's Clock and Watch Industry", Almanac of China's Economy 1982, (Beijing: Jingji Guanli Zazhishe, 1982), pp.V-60 to V-62, and State Economic Commission, Investigation and Research Section, "An Analysis of the Economic Efficiency of the Watch Industry in China", Economic Investigations, No. 1 (October 1983), pp 33-36. For a survey of the development of the world clock and watch industry since the 16th century see David Landes, "Watchmaking: A Case Study in Enterprise and Change", Business History Review, Vol. LIII, No. 1 (Spring, 1979) pp. 1-39.

7/ Figures on clock production and watch exports are incomplete. Clock production was 160,000 in 1952 and 24.4 million in 1980. The average annual growth rate from 1952 to 1981 was 19.5%. In 1982 clock output declined by 17.9%, after a rise of 14.4% in 1981. Clock exports began in 1958 and have grown from 410,000 in 1960 to 3.7 million in 1970, 5.9 million in 1975, 8.7 million in 1980, and 9.6 million in 1981. See Statistical Yearbook of China 1981 (Beijing: Zhongguo Tongji Chubanshe, 1982) and Statistical Yearbook of China 1983 (Beijing: Zhongguo Tongji Chubanshe, 1983).

8/ As in Chongqing, all clock and watch production in Shanghai is grouped under one company, the Shanghai City Clock and Watch Industrial Corporation. The Shanghai Company has 28 factories and 23,000 workers. The Company (or Corporation - both translations are used) was established in 1956, but major reorganization began in 1977. See "How We Increased Production of Clocks and Watches through Internal Adjustment", Experience of Shanghai's Industrial Enterprises, Vol. 1, (Shijiazhuang: Qiye Guanli Chubanshe, 1981), pp. 105-111.

expansion plans of many producers.[9/] Although the market for clocks is much more saturated, national production targets apparently have not been set, because clock production and prices are controlled at the provincial level.

Table 1.1: PRODUCTION OF WRISTWATCHES IN CHINA 1960-1982

Year	Production (mln watches)	Annual growth rate (%)	Imports (mln watches)	Exports (mln watches)
1960	0.5	-	0.1 /a	0
1970	3.5	21.3	0.5	0
1975	7.8	17.6	0.8	n.a. /b
1976	9.1	16.5	0.7	n.a.
1977	11.0	21.2	0.9	n.a.
1978	13.5	22.3	2.2	n.a.
1979	17.1	26.3	1.9	n.a.
1980	22.2	29.8	3.1	n.a.
1981	28.7	29.7	5.4	2.8
1982	33.0	14.9	1.0	3.5

/a 1960 was an unusual year. Imports ranged from 58,900 n 1961 to 1,662,100 in 1963. Average annual imports in 1960-69 were 540,000.

/b Watch exports started in 1973 but most probably were very small until the late 1970s.

Sources: Statistical Yearbook of China 1981 and Statistical Yearbook of China 1983.

9/ This implied average annual growth of production of 10.9% from 1982 to 1985, which has already been exceeded by the 1982 increase of 14.9%. The 1985 annual production target for CCWC was set at 1.4 million. Prior to this limitation, CCWC had been planning to produce 3 million watches by 1985. Development plans of 38 state-listed factories called for production totalling nearly 60 million watches by 1985, 33% above the national target. Planning targets in China are of varying degrees of hardness. In some industries, such as cigarettes, the target is a firm upper limit; if it is exceeded, the firm is penalized. At the other extreme, the target is set so that a moderately competent enterprise can exceed it. This was the positon of the watch industry in about 1980. The present situation appears to be an intermediate case in which watch producers are not permitted to expand their capacity beyond the target level, assuming constant productivity, but they will be permitted to exceed their target if they can increase production through improved productivity and if they can sell what they produce. It is unclear, however, whether watch production will be effectively controlled through the state plan. Localities have set up 25 factories unlisted in the state plan. These will produce an additional 3 million watches per year by 1985 if their production is unchecked. The authorities have so far been unsuccessful in controlling these factories.

1.08 Watch prices have been lowered three times since 1980, most recently in January 1983. The total reduction has amounted to over 20% of the pre-1980 price. The price set by the state is the minimum price. This appears to be done in order to protect high-cost producers and safeguard budget revenues from high taxes and profit remittances. At present, the minimum retail price for a first grade men's watch is Y 70 - still well above the average cost of Y 18 [10/] and the world price of around US$10 (Y20 at the current exchange rate). [11/] A substantial portion of the price is wholesale and retail mark-up (Y 15.80 for a first grade watch) and industrial and commercial tax (Y 21.70, or 40% of the ex-factory price), but the profit margin is still high (Y 13 for a first-grade watch in CCWC, but only Y 3-4 for a third grade watch). The price reductions were consistent with the national adjustment strategy of expanding consumption and improving living standards, but particularly the more recent changes in 1982 and 1983 were also prompted by changes in market conditions as supply caught up with demand.

1.09 The Chinese clock and watch industry has some unusual features. First, Chinese per capita production and consumption is high in relation to income (see Table 1.2). India produces fewer than 5 million watches and consumes an estimated 8 million per year. In per capita terms, China's annual consumption is more than 2 times and production 4 1/2 times that of India. China's per capita consumption is nearly three-fourths that of Malaysia, which has a much higher per capita income.

10/ Production costs in 1980 ranged from Y 11.02 for the Shanghai Watch Factory (output 4.63 million) to Y 41.37 for the Yangzhou Watch Factory in Jiangsu (output 0.26 million). CCWC's unit cost was Y 22.15 in 1980 (output 0.5 million). The costs of small factories outside the state plan (not included in the nationwide average) range as high as Y 75 and average Y 43.33. See Chapter 3 for analysis of production costs and economies of scale. Data are from State Economic Commission, Investigation and Research Section, op cit.

11/ The c.i.f. import price of Chinese watches into Thailand was $8.81 in 1979. The Chinese unit export value of watches in 1981 (from Customs Statistics, based on three-quarter average) was Y 18.04 ($10.62 at the average 1981 exchange rate). However, the Chinese unit export value fell to Y 12.01 in 1981 (for three quarters) and to Y 4.53 in 1983 (first two quarters). The recent price declines may reflect exports of low-grade mechanical watches or digital watches which could not be sold domestically.

Table 1.2: ANNUAL CONSUMPTION OF WATCHES IN SELECTED COUNTRIES

Country	Per capita income 1980 ($)	Estimated consumption of watches per capita
India	240	0.011
China	290	0.024
Kenya	420	0.006
Malaysia	1,620	0.033
United Kingdom	7.920	0.288
Japan	9.890	0.491

Source: Per capita income is from World Bank, World Development Report 1982. Consumption estimates are based on production statistics in United Nations, Yearbook of Industrial Statistics, and national foreign trade statistics. Chinese figures are from Table 1.1 and Indian figures are estimates supplied to the World Bank by industry sources.

1.10 Demand for watches is affected not only by the average level of income but also by income distribution. As incomes rise beyond a certain threshold, demand for luxury goods such as watches grows very rapidly. In China's urban areas, where incomes are relatively equally distributed, watches have become a mass consumer good, with over half the population now estimated to own a watch. In rural areas demand for watches has begun to grow rapidly as a result of large increases in rural incomes, but the level of watch ownership is still much lower than in cities.[12/]

1.11 A second contrast with the watch industry in other countries is the low level of Chinese labor productivity. Average annual output of watches per worker in China in 1981 was 524. In one of the two watch factories in India labor productivity is 909 watches per person per year, while in a Japanese factory output per worker is 16,500 watches, over 30 times the average Chinese

12/ According to the Statistical Yearbook of China 1983, 18.8% of the total population owned a watch in 1982, 10.2% of the rural population and 55.8% of urban residents. In the past Chinese watch demand may have been higher because of both the fairly equal distribution of urban incomes and the unequal distribution between urban and rural areas. At a low per capita income the most favorable income distribution from the point of view of consumer durable demand is one in which as large a percentage of the population as possible has an income just above the threshold of demand for consumer durables, subject to a constraint on minimum income for the rest of the population. As average income rises the optimum distribution moves toward greater equality.

level.[13/] This does not necessarily mean that the Chinese watch industry is inefficient compared to India and Japan. Output per worker is only a partial measure of economic efficiency even if production conditions are similar. Using labor-intensive production techniques rather than highly-automated Japanese methods may be a perfectly appropriate response to different relative factor costs. In addition, Japan produces electronic quartz watches which have only 55 components, compared to 138 components for the typical Chinese mechanical watch. In the Indian factory, 20% of output is electronic watches, while in China the share of electronic watches is very low. Finally, there is considerable variation in labor productivity (and costs) within the Chinese watch industry. Output per worker in the Shanghai Watch Factory, which produces more watches (about 5 million per year) than both Indian factories combined, was 1,052 in 1980 and 1,220 in 1981. Some of the smaller producers in China obviously have very low labor productivity; the average in the rest of the industry was only 377 watches per worker in 1981. In 1980 labor productivity in one Chinese factory was as low as 89.[14/] This is due in part to diseconomies of scale, in part to inferior management, and perhaps to other factors as well. In the Chongqing Number 1 Watch Factory, with output per worker similar to the national average, there are a few obvious economies in labor use which could be made.[15/]

1.12 The large number of producers with great differences in efficiency is a third unusual characteristic of the Chinese watch industry. China has the largest number of independent, more-or-less fully integrated watch producing firms in the world.[16/] New producers have sprung up in nearly all of China's provinces, and the majority of firms try to make most of the components and parts needed for watches themselves. Twenty-one small factories, with output of less than 500,000 watches each in 1980, accounted

---

13/ Chinese figures are from Statistical Yearbook of China 1981. Other figures are from unpublished World Bank data. National data for India and Japan are unavailable.

14/ "Brief Introduction of the Shanghai Watch Factory", Almanac of China's Economy 1982; "An Analysis of the Economic Efficiency of the Watch Industry in China."

15/ One measure would be to increase the number of automatic lathes tended by each worker. Overall efficiency (though not necessarily labor productivity) could probably be sharply raised by expanding operations from two to three shifts. Output per worker in the No. 1 Watch Factory is generously estimated: in 1982, 1,533 workers produced about 500,000 watches and 300,000 sets of components for assembly by other units. This illustrates the problems of comparing labor productivity due to possible incompatibility of definitions or coverage.

16/ It is likely that all twelve largest producers in the Chinese watch industry in 1980 were fully integrated. The smallest of them, the Chongqing Clock and Watch Company, was. A substantial number of smaller producers also may have been largely integrated.

for about 21% of total national production in that year. The share of small producers may have increased since then. Five medium-sized firms with an output of between 500,000 and 1 million watches accounted for another 16% of total national production. The large variation in production costs and labor productivity has already been documented. Variation in capital-output ratios is just as great.[17/]

1.13 In view of the apparently considerable economies of scale in watch production (see pp. 55-58) and very low transport costs (for both finished watches and parts and components), this is probably not the most economically rational industrial structure. The proliferation of small producers may be due to a number of factors: (a) adjustment policies which gave high priority to rapid expansion of consumer durables production, largely disregarding cost; (b) a desire on the part of local authorities to promote local industrialization, perhaps in part due to difficulties in obtaining supplies of consumer durables from elsewhere; (c) a tendency to establish comprehensive production even in small factories, which may be partly the result of impediments to the free flow of watch parts and components between different parts of the country; and (d) the high price of watches, which enabled even inefficient producers to earn a profit.

1.14 A fourth notable feature of the Chinese watch industry is the continued dominance of mechanical watches. In much of the world, mechanical watches have been almost completely displaced by electronic quartz watches. Official Chinese policy is to continue expanding mechanical watch production for several years.[18/] The main reason given for this is consumer resistance to electronic watches. Digital watches are almost completely unacceptable in China,[19/] but even quartz analog watches (with conventional face and hands) are unpopular because of difficulties in getting service and replacement parts.

1.15 Provided that the greater accuracy of electronic watches is not highly valued by consumers, there are good economic reasons for expecting a continued preference for mechanical watches in China. Servicing costs for mechanical watches are much lower than they are in high-wage industrialized countries, while batteries and other electronic parts are at least as costly as elsewhere. Even if watches were sold at international prices in China, it

---

17/ Production costs at factories for which data are available vary by a factor of about 4 to 1, nearly 7 to 1 in the case of certain factories not registered in the state plan. Labor productivity varies by a factor of 12-13 to 1, capital productivity by 12 to 1 (State Economic Commission, Investigation and Research Section, op cit).

18/ More specifically, "While continuing to develop mechanical clocks and watches, actively develop electronic quartz clocks and watches". See Ministry of Light Industry, "China's Clock and Watch Industry".

19/ CCWC eventually had to cut the price of a trial batch of digital watches orignally priced at Y 100 to Y 15 and even then sales have been slow.

would probably be a long time before a significant portion of the population would follow the common practice in industrialized countries of replacing rather than repairing watches. These same economic forces lend plausibility to the Chinese assumption that there will continue to be an export market for mechanical watches in poor countries for several years to come.

1.16 There is a second, policy-related reason for the slow development of electronic watches. Chinese authorities intend to build up a completely self-sufficient watch industry. They appear confident that they could insulate the domestic market from foreign competition if consumer tastes change.[20/] Furthermore, they want to discourage premature obsolescence of investment and the loss of employment which would result from encouraging a shift to electronic watches. Most important, the quality and price of Chinese electronic components are still internationally uncompetitive. Although electronic watches could be mass-produced as cheaply as mechanical watches if imported electronic components were used, China has no intention of developing the electronic watch industry on this basis.[21/]

Prereform Development and Constraints

1.17 What is now the Chongqing Clock and Watch Company began in 1952 as the Chongqing Musical Instrument Factory, producing violins and accordions. In 1963 the factory was closed down because of declining demand for musical instruments and split into three different factories, one of which was the Chongqing Clock and Watch Factory.

1.18 The Chongqing Clock and Watch Factory[22/] started with 369 workers. Clock production had begun on a modest scale in 1958 and expanded after the establishment of a separate factory to 100,000 clocks by 1969 and nearly 500,000 by 1975 (Table 1.3). In 1970 CCWC began experimental production of watches, but full-scale production was not approved until 1977. By 1979 watch production had reached 280,000 and clock production 700,000. In that year the factory for the first time participated in an experimental scheme which allowed it to retain 5% of planned profits and 20% of above-plan profits.

20/ However, the State Economic Commission, Investigation and Research Section, op. cit., cites smuggling as a problem.

21/ China's watch industry became self-sufficient in difficult mechanical components like shock absorbers well before the Indian industry, which also pursues autarchic policies. However, the cost of domestic shock absorbers is still 2.5 times the cost of imports from Switzerland, and quality is inferior according to CCWC officials. One of the most important issues of development strategy for China is the role of foreign technology: when to import, when to license, and when to pursue independent development. In the case of electronic components for watches, there are several key components for which foreign licenses are not available.

22/ For brevity we will hereafter refer to the prereform predecessor of the Chongqing Clock and Watch Company as CCWC.

Table 1.3: DEVELOPMENT OF CCWC AND PREDECESSORS 1952-82

	Gross value of output (Y mln) /a	Clock production	Watch production	Employment	Gross value of fixed assets (Y mln) /b
		-----('000 units)------			
1952	0.05			109	
1960	4.0			1,020	
1969	1.6	100		965	
1975	5.4	481	4	1.515	13.8
1976	5.7	382	9	1,746	16.8
1977	10.8	557	70	1,948	21.6
1978	20.5	654	181	2,501	22.4
1979	27.4	700	280	2,654	27.2
1980	45.9	1,000	502	3,787	31.9
1981	73.6	1,210	800	3,978	39.8
1982	64.9	542	884	4,287	63.7

/a 1952-69 values are in current prices. 1975-82 values are in constant 1970 prices.

/b Undepreciated value at original purchase price.

Source: Data provided by CCWC.

1.19 Prior to the implementation of full-scale reforms starting in 1980, CCWC faced two main constraints: (1) the prereform economic system itself, which limited the discretionary authority of enterprises in important ways; and (2) CCWC's lack of access to financial and material resources.

1.20 Lack of resources was probably more important than restrictions on autonomy in limiting the scale of CCWC's activities. It is true that in the prereform period CCWC could not make major investment decisions on its own.[23] But even if it had had the authority to do so, financial resources required to undertake investment projects would not have been available. Infusions of investment funds into CCWC were strictly controlled by supervisory authorities and additonal resources were hard to come by. CCWC's development of watch production in the 1970s is an example of this. Government capital construction grants totalling Y 17 million were provided to CCWC during this period, allowing it to establish an annual production capacity of 300,000 watches. But this phase of investment was essentially completed by 1978-79; state capital construction grants appear to have virtually ceased at that time, and without another infusion of investment funds there was no pros-

23/ For instance, investments resulting in an increase in floorspace of over 10 sq m required the approval of higher authority.

pect for further expansion in CCWC's watch production capacity.

1.21 Capital for investment was not the only resource constraint. Land was also very scarce in the Chongqing area, and CCWC had little room for expansion on its original site. Restrictions on conversion of agricultural land to industrial use were fairly severe, there was of course no market for land, and enterprises requesting land for expansion faced formidable bureaucratic hurdles.

1.22 The prereform economic system limited CCWC's discretionary authority and incentives in important ways, reinforcing the constraints imposed by lack of access to resources and national economic policy. Before the major organizational reform at the beginning of 1980, CCWC was an ordinary enterprise. As an enterprise it had little administrative authority and was subject to additional layers of bureaucratic control. CCWC was directly under the Chongqing Municipal Daily Use Consumer Goods Corporation, which in turn was supervised by the Municipal Light Industry Bureau. Other Chongqing government and Party organizations were also involved in supervising CCWC in various spheres of activity. It is not clear whether control over CCWC exercised via the plan was tight in the prereform situation; the general weakness of China's planning system during the period from the Cultural Revolution to the fall of the Gang of Four (1966-76) would argue against this. However, in many Chinese enterprises administrative controls over day-to-day operations as well as strategic decisions appear to have been more limiting in the prereform era than in the post-reform environment. National policy favoring heavy industry may also have limited CCWC's scope of discretionary authority, as well as restricting the flow of resources to the factory.

1.23 CCWC had only very weak formal incentives to increase output or improve efficiency. Material incentives for individual workers were nonexistent before the reintroduction of the bonus system in 1978. The enterprise as a unit was not allowed to retain profits before 1978. Before the reforms CCWC was not permitted to market its output directly; all production was procured by the commercial system. Nevertheless, it can be assumed that CCWC had an "expansion drive" typical of enterprises in centrally planned economies, and would have willingly expanded production and investment if given the opportunity to do so, even in the absence of financial incentives.

1.24 One other area where CCWC appears to have been tightly restricted should be mentioned: hiring of new workers that augmented the labor force (not replacement of existing workers who retire) and discipline or dismissal of poor or unsuitable workers. Restrictions in this area hindered the enterprise's ability to expand rapidly and improve labor efficiency.

1.25 On the eve of reforms, therefore, CCWC had to maneuver within a number of tight constraints: (1) very limited access to capital, land, or labor; (2) little authority to make decisions; and (3) little incentive to expand production or improve efficiency. These constraints most likely would have prevented CCWC from greatly expanding in the absence of reforms.

1.26 On the other hand, CCWC had certain resources and natural advantages which allowed it to grow rapidly once some of the above constraints were eased by reform and adjustment policies. Perhaps most important, after many years CCWC had attained the ability to mass-produce watches on a regular basis. Certain technical skills had been mastered by the workforce, production organization and coordination must have been developed to a certain extent, and required equipment (both imported and domestically produced) had been acquired. This advantage was even greater in the case of clocks, where production had been well established for over a decade.

1.27 Another "resource" which would prove useful in the period of rapid expansion immediately after the implementation of reforms was existing ties with smaller local enterprises, which processed raw materials and produced components for CCWC. These trading relationships were first begun in 1969 in the case of clocks, in 1975-76 in the case of watches. Though limited to purchases of parts and processing agreements (so no joint investment was involved), these relationships paved the way for subsequent use of closer associations with other enterprises to ease resource and market constraints.

1.28 CCWC also had a strong natural advantage in being the only major watch producer in Sichuan, China's most populous province, and the only comprehensive producer in all of Southwest China (Sichuan, Guizhou, Yunnan, and Tibet). Although these areas were relatively poor, the potential demand for watches from 170 million people was very great, once their incomes started growing as a result of adjustment policies. CCWC faced very little competition for this market from within Southwest China. If it could meet the competition from advanced producers outside the region its prospects were good. Based at least in part on its positon in Southwest China, CCWC appears to have been earmarked for rapid expansion even before the actual implementation of reforms in 1980. Indeed, this was one reason why it was chosen to participate in what was at the time the most advanced experimental reform program in China.

An Overview of Developments Since Reform

1.29 The reforms introduced on January 1, 1980, established CCWC as a corporation with authority over numerous subsidiary enterprises. CCWC was also given access to bank loans, allowed to retain a large share of its profits, and made partially responsible for its sales. These reforms both eased financial constraints and provided strong incentives to expand production. National adjustment policies begun in 1979 reinforced these effects. On the supply side, the priority given to light industry (particularly consumer durables) gave CCWC a stronger claim on investment resources. On the demand side, the rapid rise in consumption added to existing excess demand for watches, thus ensuring that CCWC's production would not initially be constrained by the market.

1.30 CCWC's development since 1980 can be divided into two distinct phases: a period of rapid expansion during 1980-81, followed by strenuous efforts to cope with emerging market difficulties beginning in 1982. Gross output nearly tripled between 1979 and 1981 as CCWC invested heavily in both clocks and watches and organized numerous joint ventures and mergers with other firms. Employment increased by 50%, while average wages per worker rose by 26%.

1.31 At the end of 1981, however, the clock market became saturated, and in response to signs of emerging over-capacity in the watch industry, national planning authorities limited CCWC's future targets for watch production to about half that planned by the company. At the same time, CCWC began having difficulty maintaining the quality of its first-grade watches. Moreover, the price of watches was lowered and overall market conditions shifted from excess demand to approximate balance or moderate excess supply. As a result, gross output fell by 12% in 1982 and the company was forced to initiate several measures to cope with the change in market conditions. In effect, CCWC changed its development strategy from quantity expansion to quality improvement and new product development.

1.32 The primary focus of this study is on the way in which reforms and changing market conditions influenced CCWC's behavior. Chapter 2 outlines the main reforms introduced in 1980 and analyzes their effects on incentives. CCWC's response to the reforms and to changing market conditions is discussed in Chapter 3. The final chapter evaluates CCWC's experience and draws some implications for future development.

2. ANALYSIS OF MAIN REFORMS

2.01 Reforms at CCWC can be divided into the following main groups: (1) organizational changes, including designation of CCWC as a corporation and establishment of joint ventures and various forms of association with other enterprises; (2) enterprise-level financial reforms, primarily the experimental incentive system replacing enterprise profit remittances with tax payments; (3) credit financing of fixed investment; (4) greater scope for CCWC to engage in sales promotion and direct marketing of its products; (5) changes in the planning system; and (6) reforms in the employment and wage system. Reforms in each of these areas will be briefly described and evaluated. Then the effects of the most important reforms on enterprise incentives and activities will be analyzed.

Changes in Organization

2.02 At the beginning of 1980 CCWC was transformed from an enterprise into an "enterprise-type industrial corporation." This meant that it retained the characteristics of an enterprise in most respects but was given greater authority in dealing with both subordinate units and government supervisory agencies. Though it occurred earlier than in other industries, the change in

CCWC's organizational form was part of a wholesale reorganization of industrial administration in Chongqing Municipality.24/

2.03 As a corporation, CCWC has built up a complex network involving 25 production, processing, and assembly units. Seven firms were merged outright to form CCWC at the beginning of 1980. In addition, CCWC developed close links with eight associated enterprises and eight joint ventures.25/ Two other enterprises maintain a purely commercial relationship with CCWC.

2.04 The joint ventures and associations were built upon trading and processing relationships started as much as a decade earlier, but they involve both significant investment by CCWC and tighter control by the company over their activities. The concrete arrangements differ in each case and can be quite complicated, but there are some common features. To varying degrees they all involve investment by CCWC and the other partner (or the latter's supervisory unit), with sharing of profits according to the respective investment shares. Each associated enterprise and joint venture has a management committee composed of representatives of the parties concerned, which is supposed to rule by consensus on major policy issues. In nearly all cases the chairman of the committee is appointed by CCWC. The director of the associated enterprise carries out the decisions of the management committee; in daily operations (production, supply, and sales), CCWC is supposed to exercise primary leadership.

2.05 The seven directly subordinate units incorporated into the company are more tightly controlled than the joint ventures. In 1983 the eight associated enterprises were also put directly under CCWC, and their ties with their former supervisory agencies (the district industrial bureaus) were severed. Though part of the general trend of shifts in industrial organization in Chongqing, this measure also reflected the desire to further strengthen CCWC's authority over these firms.

2.06 The goals of establishing CCWC as a corporation were two-fold: (1) to strengthen CCWC's ability to manage production comprehensively, in order to enable it to expand rapidly, and (2) to strengthen its position vis-a-vis supervisory organizations and reduce the amount of "petty tutelage" over its activities exercised by the latter. The change in organizational form was an important means by which the scope of the company's discretionary authority was expanded. Changes in the formal "rules of the game" under which CCWC

24/ For instance, on July 1, 1980, the Chongqing Sanxia Electric Fan United Production Enterprise was established, an amalgamation of an engine plant and nine parts factories (Economic Management, 1982 (12), p. 14). More recently, by the end of 1982 the municipality had combined municipality-run and district-run enterprises into 69 specialized corporations. (People's Daily, 1/28/83, p. 3).

25/ Most of the associated enterprises are collectively owned; all are located within Chongqing Municipality. Their status before 1983 was similar to that of the joint ventures.

operated may have been less important in actual practice than the transformation into a corporation, which gave CCWC enhanced administrative authority and removed its immediate supervisory unit (the Chongqing Daily Use Consumer Goods Corporation) from the scene. The Municipal Light Industry Bureau, which then became CCWC's immediate supervisory unit, was probably not in a position to monitor or exercise such tight control over the company's daily activities, even if it had wished to do so.

2.07 Usually in the shift from smaller to larger economic organization, there is a trade-off between the benefits of size (economies of scale, ability to pool resources, etc.) and the costs (need for larger information flows, difficulties in communication and coordination, weakened incentives). However, in the case of CCWC there may not have been such a trade-off, at least in the short run. The reason for this is that even before the reforms CCWC was extensively involved with numerous other enterprises. Thus problems of coordination and communication were already present. CCWC before the reforms did not have sufficient control over the activities of these other enterprises. By increasing its authority the reforms allowed CCWC to better coordinate production, without creating additional major disadvantages.

2.08 CCWC's motives for involvement in associations and joint ventures are complex.[26/] It seems clear that CCWC was not motivated by the profits it expected to earn from its financial investments in these enterprises, at least in the short run. Many of the joint ventures have been unprofitable, and CCWC has been forced to shore up some of them with interest-free loans or aid in other forms. On the other hand, CCWC has made considerable profits from shipments of components to these enterprises, particularly those in Yunnan and Guizhou Provinces. Watch and clock parts are traded within CCWC's network at uniform "internal prices," which are determined and periodically revised by the company.[27/] Prices of parts and components were originally set high so that relatively backward producers could cover their production costs. Until production at the associated enterprises is fully developed, CCWC ships out more components than it receives from them. In the future it is expected that trade will become more balanced, and internal prices will be uniformly reduced as production costs decrease. Thus the large profits CCWC earns from trade in components are likely to be only a temporary phenomenon.

26/ Higher level authorities often had their own reasons for promoting associations and joint ventures, and may have forced some of them on CCWC. They took the initiative, for example, in arranging closer ties between CCWC and a component factory in Beipei, a suburb of Chongqing. The motive was to rescue this firm from bankruptcy; this was successfully accomplished as a result of the association with CCWC.

27/ If a uniform state price exists for a certain good that price is used; but there are no unified state prices for watch parts and components, so CCWC can set them. Apparently information about the market prices of parts and components as well as the internal prices used by other manufacturers is readily available to CCWC.

2.09 A more important motivation for engaging in associations and joint ventures was to gain access to key resources needed for expansion. The most important of these appears to have been space.[28/] CCWC may have engaged in some associations and joint ventures in order to obtain financial resources. As a result of its joint venture in Yunnan, CCWC obtained foreign exchange from that province with which to import machinery for its own use. However, on balance CCWC has probably put more funds into joint ventures and associations than it has received directly or recouped through profits. The fact that some factories were already established as going concerns may have entered CCWC's calculations. It was usually cheaper and faster to build up existing production facilities than to construct entirely new ones.

2.10 CCWC also appears to have viewed associations as a means of getting around severe restrictions on the hiring of additional regular employees. However, this was shortsighted and appears to have backfired. The specialized skills required in watch manufacturing force new workers to undergo a period of training, regardless of whether they are taken on immediately after finishing school or are transferred from other factories. The CCWC vocational school is thus the most important source of appropriately trained labor for the company. Labor obtained through associations and joint ventures could become fully trained only after a lag, and by 1982 the change in market conditions had reduced labor requirements. CCWC has thus been saddled with excess labor.[29/]

2.11 An important rationale for links with enterprises in other provinces was access to markets. By shipping components to Yunnan and Guizhou for final assembly there, CCWC gained closer ties with the two provincial markets and prevented other, more advanced producers from making inroads. Commercial departments in Yunnan and Guizhou favored local producers in their procurement of watches; this treatment may also have carried over to some extent to CCWC's own products sold in the two provinces (particularly top quality watches, since these are not produced by either the Yunnan or the Guizhou factories). If CCWC had not engaged in these joint ventures, there was the danger that the enterprises concerned would have started cooperation with other watch producers and as a result would have become competitors of CCWC.

28/ This was a prime consideration in the establishment of the clock factory at a new site originally belonging to a commune and may also have been a factor in the association with a factory in the Beipei suburb of Chongqing, which acquired a piece of land from a commune where a workshop to manufacture shock absorbers was built.

29/ The merger with the commune to form the clock factory is the most prominent example. The original contract stipulated that the clock factory should hire 770 commune members as temporary workers, in perpetuity. Due to the collapse of the clock market the hiring of commune members was stopped when their number reached 380. However, none of the peasants already taken on were laid off. If the situation of the clock factory ever improves, CCWC is committed to start hiring additional peasants.

2.12 The final and perhaps strongest motivation was to strengthen control over the management and organization of production of parts and components. Many associations and joint ventures were built upon earlier trading and processing relationships. However, these did not give CCWC a great deal of power to coordinate production. Joint ventures, with CCWC providing some investment funds and explicitly in charge of production, supply, and marketing, permitted tighter comprehensive management by the company. The same is even more true in the case of enterprises directly incorporated into CCWC.

2.13 Since circumstances differ in each case, it is difficult to make an overall assessment of the joint ventures and associations established by CCWC. But three main points can be made: (a) During the phase of rapid expansion, these relationships probably did ease certain constraints and enabled CCWC to grow more quickly than otherwise would have been possible. However, this may not have been the most economically efficient way for CCWC to expand. (b) Many of these relationships entailed explicit or implicit long-term commitments by CCWC, which it could ill afford after market conditions changed drastically and growth slowed in 1982. (c) Despite the closer links established by joint ventures, associations, and outright mergers, many at CCWC feel the company still does not have sufficient control over the activities of subordinate enterprises.

The Tax System

2.14 Sichuan Province at the beginning of 1980 chose five state-owned industrial enterprises for participation in a new scheme involving substitution of direct tax payments for profit remittances to the Government budget. CCWC was one of the enterprises chosen. This pushed CCWC to the forefront of China's industrial reform effort, making it highly visible and at the same time giving supervisory agencies a considerable stake in its success.

2.15 The essence of the new financial incentive scheme is simple. Instead of turning over most of its profits to higher levels, CCWC is required to pay a fixed proportion (40% in 1980-82) of its total income as income tax. "Income" is defined in a peculiar way: in addition to conventionally defined profits it includes the total wage bill and collective welfare funds charged to production costs. The tax essentially is levied on value added minus depreciation, or in other words net product at factor cost. In order to clearly distinguish this tax from a conventional tax on enterprise profits, we will henceforth refer to it as a "net product tax." The remaining 60% of income is kept by CCWC, and used for the following purposes: (1) wages and collective welfare payments, which constitute a prior claim; (2) fixed investment ("development of production"); (3) individual workers' bonuses; and (4) construction of workers' housing and provision of other benefits and amenities.

2.16 There are guidelines on the amounts that can be used for each of these purposes. The wage bill is subject to a ceiling, while no more than 11% of total standard wages can be drawn for collective welfare expenditures and charged to production costs. Additional collective welfare expenses must be financed from enterprise retained profits. At least 60% of enterprise retained profits (after subtraction of wages and collective welfare expenditures charged to production costs) are supposed to be used for development of production, no more than 40% for bonuses, housing and other collective welfare payments.

2.17 CCWC also pays industrial-commercial sales tax at the rate of 40% of the ex-factory price of watches, 25% for clocks, and 5% for unassembled parts and components sold outside the company. These taxes have been in effect since long before the reforms, and payments are charged to enterprise costs (conventionally defined). New products at the stage of trial production can be exempted from industrial-commercial tax for a period of two years.[30/]

2.18 As part of the reforms CCWC was allowed to retain for its own use 70% of the basic depreciation fees on the fixed assets in its possession.[31/] Previously it had kept only 40%, turning the rest over to various higher-level authorities. Major repair funds have been retained by CCWC all along, but in 1979 the rate was raised from 2.5% to 2.9% of the original value of fixed assets per year. A provision of the reforms in Sichuan is that enterprises are permitted to combine their retained profits, retained depreciation funds, and major repair funds in a single pool for use in fixed investment.

2.19 To ameliorate the well-known problems of the so-called "ratchet effect",[32/] the net product tax rates for CCWC and the four other Sichuan pilot enterprises are fixed in advance and remain unchanged for three years. CCWC's 40% tax rate was levied in each of the three years 1980, 1981, and 1982. The principle used in setting the tax rate (the crucial variable in the whole incentive system) is simple. If performance (as measured by net product) in the current year is the same as it was in a stipulated base year,

---

30/ A circular from the Ministry of Finance and other central organizations in mid-1982 ordered an end to tax exemptions or reductions for clocks and watches as well as bicycles and sewing machines. It is not clear whether this applied to new products under trial-production (Government Finance, 1982(6), p. 10).

31/ Depreciation in China is calculated using the straight line method, based on the estimated useful life of the fixed asset concerned. Basic depreciation fees are drawn to provide funds to replenish the stock of fixed assets, while major repair funds are supposed to be used for overhauls and major maintenance. For CCWC the basic depreciation rate is 4.5% of the original value of its fixed assets in use per year. This rate was set in 1953 and has remained unchanged since then.

32/ The "ratchet effect" occurs when targets are frequently revised in the light of actual performance. This causes enterprises deliberately to perform more poorly than they otherwise would, in order to generate lower, easier-to-achieve targets in the future. This has been extensively discussed in the scholarly literature on centrally planned economies; for a simple theoretical model see Weitzman, Martin L., "The 'Ratchet Principle' and Performance Incentives," The Bell Journal of Economics, Spring 1980, pp. 302-308.

the amount of funds going to the enterprise should be the same as it was in the base year. If performance turns out to be better the enterprise will receive more funds, if performance is worse it will receive less. This principle is common to most of China's enterprise-level reform programs. In the case of CCWC the base year chosen was 1979. The sum of 1979 retained profits, wages, collective welfare funds drawn from production costs, and the state grant for development of new products 33/ was divided by the sum of total profits, wages, and collective welfare funds and then subtracted from one to derive the appropriate income tax rate.

2.20 However, the principle described here seems to have been rather loosely applied in practice. For instance, the appropriate tax rate with 1979 as a base year would have been 42%. But in order to "provide some additional help to CCWC," the rate was actually set at 40%. In choosing the 1983-85 tax rate it would not make much sense to use the original principle and 1982 as the base year, for the obvious reason that this would result in exactly the same 40% tax rate as before. All organizations concerned recognized the need to take into account CCWC's greatly expanded production and increased profits in setting the 1983-85 rate. However, there has been disagreement about the exact rate, with the Chongqing Municipal Tax Bureau favoring a rate of 50% and CCWC, the municipal Economic Commission, and the municipal Light Industry Bureau suggesting a rate of 44%. The final decision will be made by municipal authorities, but the company believes that it will be close to 44%. Thus the tax rate is determined at least in part by negotiations among relevant supervisory agencies, with the outcome favoring CCWC.

2.21 CCWC also gained a considerable advantage from the choice of 1979 as the base year. The company had certain resources and advantages which had not been fully utilized in 1979 (see Chapter 1). Moreover, it was on an early part of the "learning curve" in watch manufacturing; large increases in output and profits could be expected as workers became more experienced and production became more smoothly managed, as part of the natural course of events. Furthermore, there was probably much underutilized equipment which could be made more productive quickly by means of relatively small new investments. Using 1979 as the base year resulted in a low tax rate, which allowed the enterprise to receive more of the benefits from the rapid expansion which occurred subsequently. In contrast, the financial incentive scheme for an enterprise which had already achieved most of its potential in terms of production and profitability would be considerably less attractive. 34/

33/ The fund for development of new products was previously provided as a government grant but after the reforms was paid for by the enterprise itself.

34/ The Chongqing No. 3 Printing Factory, one of the four other Sichuan enterprises participating in the tax experiment, may be a good example. Its income tax rate was set at 60% (indicating greater profitability at the outset). However, its subsequent expansion has been much slower than that of CCWC.

Credit Financing of Fixed Investment

2.22 This innovation involves aspects of both system reform and adjustment policies. Credit financing of investment is supposed to encourage enterprises to economize on their use of capital by making them pay for it. At the same time, short- and medium-term equipment loans from the People's Bank of China (which accounted for most of CCWC's borrowing in 1980-82) were the main vehicle by which investment resources were channelled into China's light and textile industries during the adjustment period.

2.23 The interest rate on these loans is relatively low, but the short maturities generally not exceeding three years mean that the amortization burden is heavy and that large payments are required shortly after the loan is made. This feature would seem to make borrowing an unattractive alternative to self-financed investment for enterprises. However, it is offset by the provisions on loan repayment, which impart to these loans some of the characteristics of fiscal allocations. Loans are supposed to be repaid from the incremental benefits earned by the investment project financed by the loan. The first source of funds for repayment is incremental profits; if these are insufficient (in most cases they will not be enough because of the short repayment period), basic depreciation charges on fixed assets created by the loan-financed project and fixed asset taxes on the same can be diverted to loan repayment. If funds are still insufficient for repayment, industrial-commercial tax on the additional goods produced by the project can be diverted to this purpose. A final key feature of the system is that both principal and interest repayments by CCWC on bank loans for fixed investment are deducted from income before net product tax is calculated. This is different from normal practice in most other countries.

2.24 As part of the reforms CCWC was required to pay a tax on fixed assets in its possession and in use, starting in 1980. The tax rate is 2.52% of the original value of fixed assets per year; the tax is levied in addition to depreciation fees and loan amortization (if any). Starting in 1982, CCWC began paying a fee on its state-allocated circulating assets.[35/] Payments for both types of asset levies are subtracted from income before net product tax is calculated. The deduction of asset fees from taxable income is an unusual feature of the pilot program CCWC participates in; in most of the other 450-odd enterprises in China that experimented with the substitution of tax payments for profit delivery, asset fees (though not loan repayments) were subtracted from enterprises' after-tax retained funds.[36/] The incentives

35/ CCWC all along has paid interest on circulating assets financed by bank loans. In 1982 interest rates on these types of loans were raised, and the company participated in an experimental "floating interest rate" scheme. Excessive usage of working capital was supposed to be penalized by levying higher interest rates, while good performance in this area (low levels of inventories and circulating capital usage) was rewarded by lower interest charges.

36/ This is also true of the other 44 enterprises under the Chongqing

generated by the tax and loan repayment provisions will be analyzed later in this chapter.

Sales Promotion and Marketing

2.25 Since 1980 CCWC has been allowed to market part of its total output of clocks and watches. The company has set up 40 local retail outlets at which its products are sold directly to consumers; at the same time it also sells some products to lower-level commercial wholesale stations both inside and outside of Sichuan Province. This bypasses the "official" commercial intermediary, the Chongqing branch of the Sichuan provincial second-level wholesale station for general consumer goods, which still accounts for the majority of CCWC's total sales of both clocks and watches. Direct marketing is authorized for all of CCWC's above-plan output, as well as a stipulated percentage of within-plan output. In 1982 about 30% of CCWC's output of watches was marketed directly by the company, 6.8% at retail and the rest to other commercial units.

2.26 The goal of permitting CCWC to market some of its output was to make the company more dependent on and responsive to market conditions. It was hoped that this would generate improvements in quality, greater attention to customer needs, better warranties and repair service, greater efforts at sales promotion, and development of new products and varieties to meet market needs. It was also hoped that CCWC would expand rapidly in response to market demand. Since there was to be very little reform of the pricing system, these benefits of greater responsiveness to the market were supposed to come from the enterprise operating subject to fixed prices. The extent to which these benefits are realized depends crucially on the demand-supply situation in the market, which will be analyzed later in this chapter.

Changes in the Planning System

2.27 Changes in the way in which CCWC's economic activities are planned have been an integral part of the reforms. CCWC has been given the power to plan its production and is supposed to let output be determined by demand. Related to this, CCWC plays a significant role in planning its sales and is allowed to sign sales contracts directly with commercial units at its own discretion. On the supply side the company is allowed to arrange for its needs directly with suppliers when these exceed its input allocation quotas. CCWC also can make its own investment and financial plans.

2.28 CCWC thus has considerable ability to plan and arrange its activities, but the supervisory administrative apparatus still grinds out plan targets for the enterprise, with little or no change in the way such targets are determined. Under the present system CCWC has four mandatory targets: physical output of main products, product quality, labor productivity of

---

Municipal Light Industry Bureau, all of which became involved in an income tax scheme starting in 1981, and of the nationwide income tax system, which began to be implemented in 1983. In the new nationwide system, the tax is based on profits rather than net product.

employees, and profit.[37/] Labor is still allocated by higher authorities. In addition contracts to supply watches and clocks to the commercial system must be fulfilled. Input allocation quotas are also still assigned, but since the clock and watch industry consumes few scarce materials input quotas have never constrained CCWC's production. Fulfillment of plan targets remains important since in principle it is required in order for workers' bonuses to be paid. The output and quality targets must be fulfilled if any worker bonuses at all are to be paid. Failure to meet the profit target or inability to fulfill supply contracts would lead to a reduction in workers' bonuses.

2.29 Planning control of CCWC has been slack for many years. Targets have been set low or revised downwards if it appeared the original targets could not be fulfilled. Many plan targets have been overfulfilled by substantial margins year after year. For example, plan targets for gross industrial output value at constant prices were overfulfilled in every year since 1975, except for 1976.[38/] The margin of overfulfillment ranged from 11% to 61%, but was less than 20% in only two years. Only in 1976 were important plan indicators not fulfilled *ex post*. In 1980-82 CCWC fulfilled not only its four mandatory targets but all of its indicative targets as well.

2.30 Revision of at least some targets appears easy. For example, in 1982 the criteria originally set for bonus payments included targets for output of clocks and watches. In view of the deteriorating market situation for clocks, in June 1982 CCWC asked that 1982 bonuses be determined solely by indices for watch output. This request was promptly granted. On the other hand, unified national quality standards for watches had to be met and apparently could not be lowered; this forced CCWC to make extra efforts to improve quality in 1982.

2.31 Other than the fairly weak link between plan fulfillment and workers' bonuses, there is no formal direct relationship between mandatory plans set by higher level authorities and enterprise rewards or incentives. (This after all is the very purpose of a fixed proportional taxation system.) Even more significant, the actual process of plan determination seems not to have impinged on CCWC's decisions and activities greatly. Only annual plans are set by supervisory organizations - short-term plans are made

---

37/ Other state-owned industrial enterprises in China may have eight mandatory targets: the four given to CCWC, plus varieties or product mix, input consumption, production cost, and usage of circulating capital. CCWC also has indicative (non-mandatory) targets. These include indicators such as input consumption, which is used for internal evaluation, and gross value of output, which is derived in part from the mandatory targets for physical output of main products but is no longer itself a mandatory target. Before 1978 gross value of output was effectively the main mandatory target for Chinese enterprises.

38/ In 1982 the original plan target was not reached, but the target was revised downward by over 20%. As a result, the revised quota was overfulfilled by nearly 11%.

by CCWC for its own use. Control figures handed down are not very disaggregated.39/ Moreover, CCWC can arrange its activities in accordance with its own plans and market forecasts, even if these differ greatly from the control figures set by higher levels. For instance, in 1983 CCWC has made arrangements to produce 1-1.2 million watches and hopes to make 300,000 clocks, depending on the market situation. The state control figures for 1983 are 900,000 watches and 500,000 clocks. Based on its past experience, CCWC expects that the control figures will be changed in the last quarter of 1983 to conform with its actual performance.40/

2.32 Although CCWC's annual production planning is little affected by the higher level planning apparatus, this may no longer be true of investment decisionmaking. The threat of oversupply in the watch market forced central authorities to set fixed production targets for all watch producers. As a result, CCWC has had to curtail some investment plans. Even in this case, however, it appears that CCWC will be allowed to exceed its 1985 production control figure, provided that it does this by improving labor productivity rather than expanding capacity and that it can readily market the additional watches.

Reforms in the Employment and Wage System

2.33 Labor allocation is the least reformed part of the system. Quotas largely unrelated to the production plan still limit the number of workers CCWC can hire. Lazy or inefficient workers are rarely penalized, let alone dismissed. Redundant workers cannot be laid off. When several hundred workers were made redundant by the collapse of the clock market in 1982, the worst that happened was that groups of 300 workers at a time were placed on study leave with temporary loss of bonus.41/ CCWC also has little control over selection of particular workers, though the company can give limited preference to children of workers who pass apprenticeship or the company's Technical School entrance exams.42/ Lack of control over total employment and

---

40/ There is one target for number of clocks produced and one for watches. Product mix within the two categories is determined by CCWC in consultation with the commercial unit that purchases its output.

40/ However, CCWC feels more constrained by its profit target, which appears to be more difficult to revise. The 1982 clock production target could be revised easily in part because the profit target did not have to be revised.

41/ In 1983, however, CCWC will not permit any bonus to be paid to clock workers unless the Clock Factory makes a profit. Moreover, 20% of basic wages will also depend on meeting the factory profit target. Some workers have been forced to sell a certain number of clocks on their own or lose part of their salary. See p. 50.

42/ About half of apprentices and entrants to the Technical School (set up in 1978 to train skilled workers) are children of workers. As a general

individual worker selection and discipline was the main remaining dissatisfaction voiced by CCWC management.

2.34 Bonuses for individual workers were restored in 1978 and expanded in 1980. Bonuses equivalent to 2.5 months' average basic wages can be paid and charged to production costs if CCWC meets its four mandatory planning targets and fulfills all economic contracts.43/ In theory, 10% of total retained profits were also supposed to have been available for additional bonuses during 1980-82, but CCWC was never permitted to use the stipulated share of profits for bonuses. Because of resentment by workers in other factories, municipal authorities instructed CCWC to use the bonus fund for collective welfare payments instead. However, there is a director's fund financed from retained profits and equivalent to 3% of the wage bill which can be used for special bonuses such as those for labor competition, product development, technical innovation, and cost reduction.

2.35 Bonuses are not very closely linked to performance, either of the enterprise as a whole or of individual workers. Slack planning enables targets to be easily met or revised, thus weakening the link between bonuses and overall performance. Individual incentives are weak because bonuses are distributed on a fairly egalitarian basis. Since targets and related bonuses are handed down to factories, workshops, and small groups, an individual's bonus payment depends as much on his work unit's performance as on his own. Only small variations between work units have occurred in the past,44/ and differences within factories are even smaller; about 70% of workers receive bonuses within a very narrow range.45/ Only about half the bonus fund for labor competition was distributed to individual workers in 1982. The remainder was handed out equally to all workers at the end of the year. Other bonuses have also been shared out equally. CCWC's management has the authority to differentiate individual bonuses more than it has done so far.

2.36 The pressure for egalitarianism appears to come mainly from the workers themselves. The unpopularity of sharp differentiation among individuals is illustrated by the failure of a piece-rate wage system tested in 1981. Productivity increased, but the system was withdrawn mainly because workers found that the slight advantage of the additional average income

---

rule in China, a retiring worker's child can "inherit" the retiree's job.

43/ This is a national ceiling for state enterprises. In 1981 the ceiling was 3 months' basic salary.

44/ Clock factory workers received an average bonus equal to 2 months' basic wages in 1982, compared to a company average of 2.5 months.

45/ The distribution of annual bonuses among the 19 factory directors and assistant directors in the 7 factories directly under CCWC in 1982 was as follows: the lowest bonus paid was Y 50 and the highest "over Y 90", with 70% receiving a bonus of Y 80. Average bonuses paid to manual workers are 25-35% higher than managerial bonuses, but the variability is said to be similar.

afforded by piece rates was more than offset by harder work and greater differentiation in incomes among small groups and individual workers.[46/]

2.37 Two other changes in the wage and benefit system have had a more significant impact on worker motivation. Both function largely as group incentives for all the company's workers.

2.38 The first of these is a new "floating wage" system introduced in 1981, whereby workers can be temporarily paid a wage rate higher than that stipulated for their wage grade. Under this system, Y 1.50 per worker per month can be put into a "wage adjustment fund" to finance floating wage increases, provided all mandatory targets are met. The fund is increased by Y 0.10 per worker per month for every 3% overfulfillment of the profit target, up to a limit of Y 1.95. At the end of the year, the fund can be used to finance a provisional wage grade increase for a specified percentage of workers.[47/] This provisional or floating increase will be confirmed as a permanent increase if company performance is maintained the following year and revoked if company performance worsens. At the end of 1981, 76% of CCWC workers received a floating wage increase. In 1982 only 20% of the labor force qualified for a wage grade increase because company performance worsened, but all but 7 workers who received the floating increase in 1981 were to be confirmed in their new grade in early 1983. Although the amount of money involved may seem small, since this is a permanent wage increase and since wage grade promotions in China are rare, the benefit is actually quite large.[48/]

2.39 The second group incentive provided by the reforms in CCWC is the collective welfare benefits financed from a share of retained profits. Of total retained profits of Y 13.3 million during 1980-82, about 60% have gone to collective welfare benefits, with the lion's share used to build apartments for families of 334 workers.[49/] CCWC's labor force feels an acute shortage of housing. Only workers who joined the company in 1970 or before have been

---

46/ Chinese workers are not unique in their dislike of piece rates, of course.

47/ CCWC has its own wage grade system with 15 grades for manual workers instead of the usual 8. Grade increments are smaller (about Y 4 per month in the middle ranges), but the range of wages is similar to the 8 grade system.

48/ The present value of a Y 4.00 per month increase (one wage grade promotion), assuming a 5% discount rate and an additional working life of 25 years, is Y 676, compared to the average wage (including bonuses) per permanent worker in 1982 of Y 884.

49/ Regulations stipulate that only 30% of retained profits can be used for collective welfare. The 10% share designated for bonuses could also be used for collective welfare when, as in CCWC's case, bonus payments were restricted.

allocated apartments by CCWC. Company housing is valued because rents are highly subsidized (they do not even cover the cost of ordinary maintenance) and because once allocated to a worker a flat virtually belongs to him and his heirs for as long as they maintain continuous occupation. The only means of obtaining company housing is through CCWC's continued retention of large amounts of profits.[50/]

The Company's Objective Function

2.40 The impact of the new incentive system implemented by CCWC depends very much on the objectives the enterprise actually pursues. We will argue that CCWC has striven to maximize the family income of its workers. Because of CCWC's special circumstances and constraints, this is roughly equivalent to maximizing the sum of its retained profits and wages (or net product for short). Other possible maximands include: (a) personal benefits of managers; (b) degree of fulfillment of enterprise performance targets; (c) profits, and (d) average net product per worker. Each of these alternatives is discussed below.

2.41 It is commonly assumed in analysis of enterprise management in the Soviet Union and Eastern Europe that managers maximize some narrowly construed function of their present and future earnings (salaries and bonuses), including benefits from future promotions and transfers. This approach is inappropriate in China for several reasons. Managerial bonuses are small and do not vary much with enterprise or individual performance. Salaries are fixed; promotions tend to be relatively infrequent and are based on many factors in addition to individual performance. Finally, turnover is low for managers as well as workers. Although managers may not spend their entire working lives in one enterprise as most workers do, many of them will spend long periods of time at a single firm. As a result they are likely to identify closely with the long-term performance of their units and the welfare of their workers, particularly since enterprise performance depends on worker morale.

2.42 It is also difficult to believe that the enterprise maximizes some function of the performance targets set by outside authorities. If it did, it is unlikely that CCWC would have made so many efforts to manipulate and distort the incentive system in 1980-82. In addition, the planning system is so slack and targets are so easily revised that fulfillment of performance targets has little meaning.

2.43 Profit maximization, the conventional motivational assumption in models of capitalist enterprise behavior, appears at first glance to provide a better explanation of CCWC's behavior. Reforms have given CCWC control over a large amount of discretionary funds, and the company has made strong efforts

---

50/ In the prereform period, housing for workers (such as there was) was financed by state capital construction grants. With the implementation of reforms, however, firms that retain profits are supposed to pay for workers' housing construction themselves, and government grants for this purpose have been discontinued.

to increase retained profits through output expansion, new product development, and manipulation of its administrative and incentive environment. However, under existing Chinese labor market conditions a profit-maximizing firm would probably try to restrict increases in wages, bonuses, and worker amenities. CCWC by contrast has often tried to increase worker benefits. Much of the company's effort to manipulate the rules on calculation and use of retained income has been devoted to trying to increase workers' bonus or collective welfare payments.

2.44 CCWC's attempts to increase direct worker benefits suggests that it was concerned with both wages and profits, but this still leaves open the question whether the company wished to maximize average net product per worker or total net product. It is normally assumed that the maximand of labor-managed firms, such as those in Yugoslavia, is average net product per worker.[51/] In this model firms are concerned only with benefits to existing workers. They will wish to expand employment only if the marginal net product of a new worker exceeds the average net product of existing workers, because only then will expansion raise incomes of existing workers. If completely unconstrained, Chinese firms might conform to this model. However, binding upper limits on workers' wages and bonuses are generally imposed from outside, so that firms are effectively prevented from increasing benefits per worker beyond a certain point. This suggests that the firms will cease to be interested in expanding output once allowable worker benefits have been attained.

2.45 CCWC had strong reasons, however, for wanting to expand employment and output beyond the point at which workers received the maximum allowable bonus. One important factor was the shortage of (highly subsidized) company housing. Housing was allocated by seniority, and only a minority of workers had received it. A large share of retained profits could be used to build housing, which gave CCWC's workers a strong interest in expanding company profits. The motivation was strongest for those workers next on the eligibility list, of course, but even workers who already had housing would be interested in the company's profitability if their own children were working in CCWC and still living at home.[52/] In this situation existing workers would not be opposed to hiring additional laborers since this would not lower their own incomes and might (through expansion of production and an increase in profits) speed up the allocation of housing to them or to their children living at home.

2.46 Two other special features of CCWC's situation contributed to its

---

51/ See, for example: Benjamin Ward, "The firm in Illyria: Market Syndicalism," American Economic Review, Vol. 58, No.4 (September 1958), pp. 566-589; James Meade, "The Theory of the Labor-Managed Firm and of Profit Sharing," Economic Journal, Vol. 82, No. 325 S. (March 1972), pp. 402-428.

52/ About 1,500 workers at CCWC live with their parents and half of these are children of company workers.

motivation to expand output. First, the floating wage scheme provided a direct link between wages and profits which was absent in many other firms. Second, the fact that about half of the increment to CCWC's labor force consisted of dependents of existing workers would also cause the latter to look favorably upon new hiring.

2.47 In summary, CCWC's objective function is perhaps best approximated by total net product.53/ Other firms in China do not necessarily have the same objective function as CCWC. A firm's objective function depends on its particular circumstances and on the constraints under which it operates. The desire to obtain workers' housing was a prime force behind CCWC's expansion drive, but other enterprises may have quite different interests. Moreover, there is an interaction between the objective function and rules or incentives. If CCWC were allowed to distribute all profits as bonuses rather than as collective welfare expenditure or investment, or if the company could no longer hire children of existing workers, it might well prefer to maximize average rather than total net product. Similarly, changes in rules governing management appointments and rewards or increased tautness of plans could also change the enterprise's objective function and hence its behavior.

2.48 Under current rules and conditions, there are strong grounds for believing that most Chinese enterprises have an objective function which depends on both the discretionary funds available to managers and the income accruing to workers. In the case of CCWC during 1980-82, the relevant objective function appears to have been total net product. The objective function postulated implicitly assumes that all the main components are weighted equally; an extra yuan in retained profits is worth exactly the same to the enterprise as an extra yuan of bonuses or an extra yuan of wages to new workers. There is no *a priori* reason to believe the weights should be fixed, let alone equal to each other. This assumption is made only in the interest of simplicity.

Incentives Created by Financial Reforms

2.49 Individual reforms cannot be studied in isolation. The incentives generated by a particular reform depend on the firm's objective function, the constraints it faces, and the interactions of different reforms with each other. This section will analyze the main incentives created by the tax, investment financing, and marketing reforms and the interactions among them.

2.50 The main incentive effect of the new tax system is that CCWC shares in a much higher proportion of the profits earned by its activities. At the margin it keeps 60% of its profits. This compares with 20% of incremental profits it kept in 1979 under an earlier pilot scheme, and no profit retention at all before the reforms.

53/ Strictly speaking, the floating wage scheme and the link between profits and housing imply that workers would want to maximize profits. However, total family income of workers might be increased through hiring of dependents even if employment expansion reduced profits.

2.51 One unusual feature of CCWC's tax is that all of net product - both profits and wages - is taxed. The resulting incentives depend on the firm's objective function. Without a tax, or with a conventional profit tax, a profit-maximizing firm will expand employment and output as long as the marginal product of a new worker exceeds the wage rate. But with a tax on both wages and profits, a profit-maximizing firm will seek to substitute capital for labor and will only employ new workers so long as their marginal product exceeds the wage plus tax rate. A labor-managed firm striving to maximize average net product is affected differently; it will always be more restrictive in hiring than a profit maximizing firm because it will only wish to expand if the marginal product of a new worker exceeds the average net product of existing workers. A tax on both wages and profits will not make the labor-managed firm less willing to expand than it already was, however, because it reduces both existing and incremental net product equally. Finally, a firm with CCWC's assumed objective function (maximization of total net product) will be very expansionist under all conditions.[54/] Such a firm will seek to increase employment so long as the marginal product of labor is greater than zero and the net product tax will have no effect on this incentive. However, a profit tax on a firm which maximizes net product would create an incentive to raise wages or employment until profits are reduced to zero. Since only profits are taxed, the firm could even expand after-tax net product by employing labor with negative marginal product. In brief, the net product tax has a neutral incentive effect because net product is the maximand. More generally, to be neutral a tax should cover the base which the firm is trying to maximize.

2.52 Since the net product tax has a broader base than a profit tax, for a given tax yield in the initial year it also has a lower tax rate. The changes in incentives this generates are too complex to analyze in detail, but two particular effects should be noted. First, the net product tax gives a stronger incentive than a profit tax to reduce material costs of production, because the retention rate from incremental profits created by savings in material costs is higher. (By the same token the net product tax provides no incentive to reduce labor costs, but of course a firm maximizing total net product has no incentive to reduce labor costs in any case.) Second, the net product tax implies a higher risk for labor. Under a profit tax, if profits disappear tax liability is reduced to zero. Under a net product tax, labor will still be taxed even if a firm is making a financial loss.

54/ The marginal product of new workers was so high during 1980-81 that CCWC would have had a strong incentive to expand employment whatever its objective function. The average wage of a regular worker in 1979 was Y 706 (rising to Y 929 in 1981). Net product (wages plus retained profit) per regular worker increased from Y 922 in 1979 to Y 2,868 in 1981, but fell to Y 1,506 in 1982. Thus the data for these years do not permit a decisive test of alternative hypotheses. However, the company's behavior in 1980-82 (see Chapter 3) was mostly consistent with the motivation to maximize total net product.

2.53 The introduction of credit financing of fixed investment was intended to give Chinese enterprises a greater incentive to conserve capital than existed under the old system of grant finance. However, unusual tax deduction features (by Western standards) have caused strange and probably unintended incentive effects.

2.54 Under grant financing, enterprises were required to hand over not only profits but also a high proportion of depreciation allowances to the state. Fixed asset fees were also introduced to create an incentive to conserve capital provided by the state. Although CCWC's retention of depreciation funds was raised from 40% to 70% when grant financing was discontinued under the reforms, the basic principle that CCWC should hand over part of depreciation fees and pay a fixed asset tax was applied to new investment as well as existing grant financed capital. Both of these provisions tax capital and hence lower the rate of return on investment and create an incentive to substitute labor for capital. This tends to offset existing biases in the system. Because of price distortions, the rate of return on investment in light industry is very high. Decentralized investment decisions based on high, fixed prices would lead to excess investment and a tax on capital tends to offset this distortion. Similarly, it can be argued that industrial wages exceed the opportunity cost of labor while capital prices are generally below the shadow cost of production. A capital tax thus may help offset the bias in relative factor prices. But even if one concedes that there is a certain second-best logic to taxing capital in this way, there is no evidence that rates of depreciation retention and fixed asset tax bear much relation to product and factor price distortions.

2.55 Moreover, most of the impact of the capital tax is offset for credit-financed investment by loan repayment provisions. This makes credit financing much more attractive than self-financing. Because CCWC is allowed to deduct both principal and interest paid from incremental profits before paying income tax, 40% of the principal amount of a loan is in fact a grant to CCWC, since it consists of money that would otherwise have been turned over to the government. The diversion of other funds to loan repayment makes loan financing even more attractive. Loan repayment is to be made from the incremental benefits of the project, in the following order: profits, depreciation charges, fixed asset tax, and industrial-commercial tax. CCWC retains for its own use 70% of depreciation funds, so their diversion to loan repayment does entail a considerable loss to CCWC. This is not true of fixed asset taxes and industrial-commercial tax, however. If these sources are dipped into for loan repayment, then the enterprise ends up paying considerably less than 60% of the cost of loan-financed projects. This is fairly likely since the maturity of loans is very short (generally not more than three years), meaning that incremental profits alone may be insufficient to fully amortize them.

2.56 Perhaps more important than the <u>level</u> of the benefits to the enterprise is their <u>distribution</u> with respect to uncertain outcomes. This is important because enterprise decisionmakers are risk averse, with respect to their personal situations as well as that of the enterprise. Attitudes toward risk are especially important in considering technological innovation and development of new products, which are inherently risky activities.

2.57 The most striking feature of the mode of repayment of fixed investment loans in this context is that the enterprise bears none or only a part of the financial risks of the project. This is illustrated by Figure 2.1. The vertical axis shows benefits accruing to the enterprise as a result of the project, in the form of retained profits and wages, while the horizontal axis measures the incremental benefits of the project, including total profits, depreciation funds, fixed asset fees, and industrial-commercial tax. The line AE gives enterprise benefits as a function of total project benefits. The different segments of the line correspond to different rates at which the enterprise and the government share in the risks and benefits of the project, depending on which funds are being used for loan repayment.

2.58 The segments AB and A'B correspond to the range where total project benefits (as defined here) as are so low that even combined they are insufficient to repay the loan. The regulations do not say exactly what would happen in this case. If the additional payments come from CCWC's profits earned from other activities, the segment AB is the appropriate one. The enterprise assumes 60% of the marginal risk in this case, because 40% of the profits used for repayment otherwise would be paid as income tax.[55/]

2.59 On the other hand, the enterprise's supervisory agency (the Chongqing Municipal Light Industry Bureau in the case of CCWC) might undertake to repay the loan with its own funds or at least divert other funds to this purpose. In this case the segment A'B is the appropriate one and there is a clear floor, below which enterprise benefits from the project will not fall. This corresponds to the additional wage payments to enterprise employees generated by the project.[56/]

2.60 The segment BC covers the range of project benefits over which total benefits are sufficient to repay the loan, but incremental profits and depreciation funds are not. In this case the marginal loan repayment comes from the fixed asset tax or industrial-commercial tax, which does not affect what the enterprise gets. Over the range BC (or A'C) the enterprise does not share in the risks of the project at all, but receives project benefits in lump-sum form (additional wages).

2.61 The segment CD corresponds to the range of benefits where the marginal repayment comes from depreciation funds. Since the enterprise would otherwise be allowed to keep 70% of these funds for its own use, it shares in 70% of the marginal benefits and risks of the projects. In the range of project benefits corresponding to DE, the level of benefits is so high that the entire loan can be repaid from incremental profits alone (of which the

---

55/ This assumes that profits from other activities are sufficient to cover loan repayments.

56/ If the firm maximizes retained profits, the floor would be located along the horizontal axis, that is, the line A'C would be shifted down to the horizontal axis. The distance OA' corresponds to the additional wage payments generated by the project.

Figure 2.1: BENEFIT SCHEDULE FOR LOAN-FINANCED FIXED INVESTMENT PROJECT

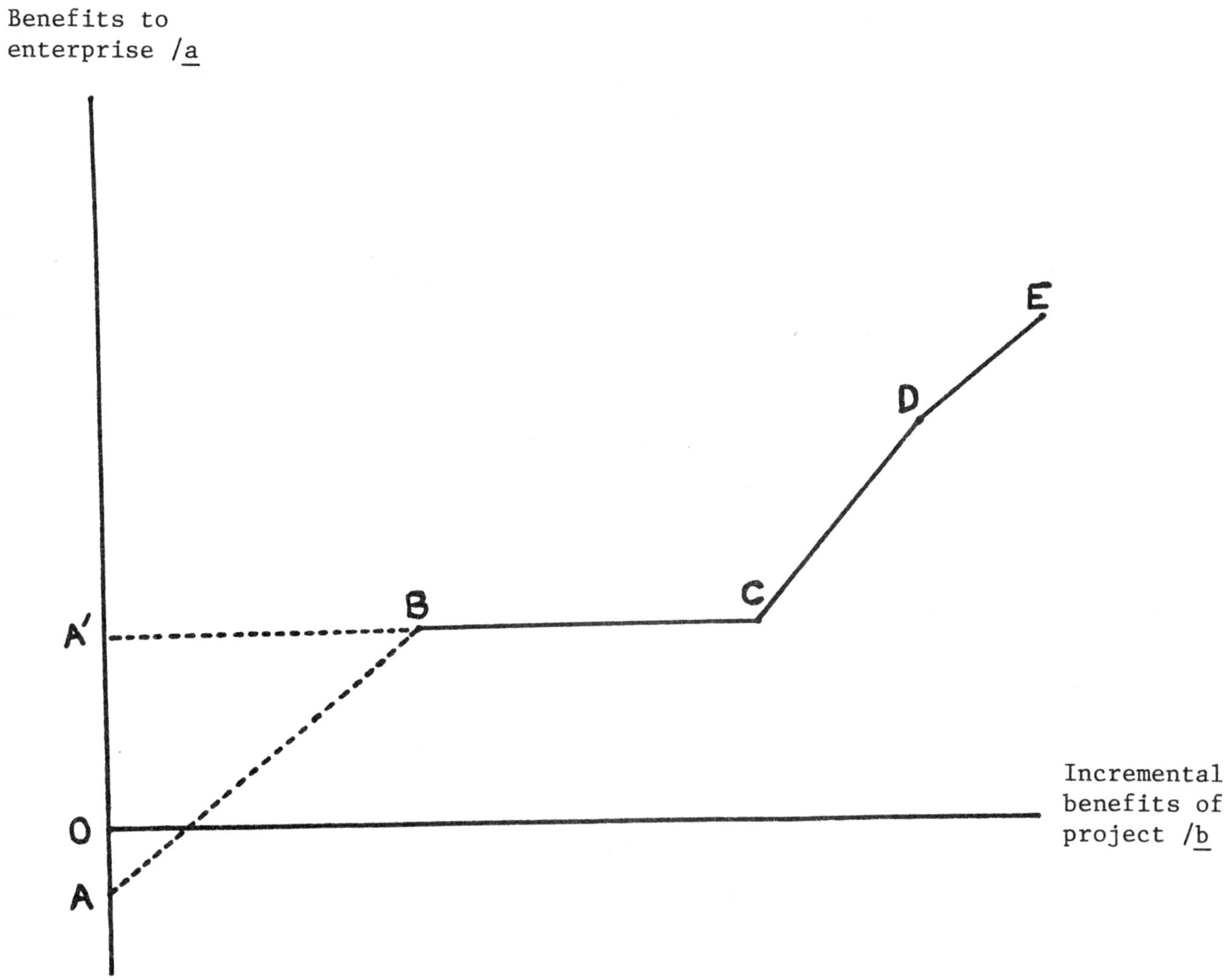

/a Sum of enterprise-retained profits and wage costs.

/b Sum of incremental profits, depreciation funds, fixed asset tax, and industrial-commercial tax.

enterprise would otherwise give 40% to the government and keep 60%). Due to the short maturity of the loans very few projects are likely to be in this position.

2.62 The overall net effect of all the tax payments, depreciation charges, and tax deductions depends on the profitability of the investment, loan repayment terms and time preference rate used. Nevertheless, it is possible to draw some broad conclusions. In comparison to the typical Western accounting and tax procedures (in which all depreciation funds are retained by the firm, no asset tax is paid and only interest payments are deductible from taxable income), the system applied to CCWC generally: (1) lowers the net cash flow from self-financed investment and (2) raises the net cash flow from investment financed by loans. In other words, CCWC's self-financed investment is taxed and its loan-financed investment is subsidized, compared to a Western tax and accounting system.

2.63 The new tax system gave CCWC an incentive to increase net product, and the complicated system of capital taxes and deductions made borrowing more attractive than self-financed investment. A third reform giving CCWC increased responsibility for marketing affected the direction of efforts to increase net product, i.e., the incentive to engage in extensive or intensive growth. The former involves growth of output with equal growth of inputs, and little if anything in the way of quality improvements, development of new products, or improvements in efficiency (cost reductions). The latter can mean growth of output without commensurate growth of factor or material inputs, as well as quality improvement, development of new products, and substantial improvement of technology.

2.64 The direction of effort towards extensive or intensive growth depends crucially on the demand-supply situation in the market. Since the reforms did not affect price setting, prices were generally fixed by the state at a level which reflected neither short-run nor long-run market equilibrium. Assume that the enterprise takes state-set prices as given and that prices are high enough that production is profitable. If there is excess demand in the market (the fixed price is below the short-run equilibrium price), both a profit maximizing firm and one maximizing net product will expand production. However, there is little if any incentive to improve quality, engage in costly sales promotion, develop new products, or provide better services to customers. With excess demand in the marketplace, the firm can sell whatever it produces without taking such measures. On the contrary, the enterprise has incentives to adulterate quality, provide poor service to customers, and continue producing obsolete goods. Thus few if any of the desired benefits of reliance on the market mechanism are realized if there is chronic excess demand.

2.65 The situation changes radically if the market is in rough equilibrium or if there is excess capacity. The enterprise can no longer take its ability to sell all of its output for granted. In order to sell what it produces, it must meet competition from other producers. Since the fixed price regime prevents overt price competition, various forms of nonprice competition are restorted to. There will be a natural tendency for producers to improve quality, provide better services to customers, develop new products and more stylish varieties, and engage in sales promotion. Thus the benefits desired from greater reliance on the market mechanism can be realized if there is excess supply or at least rough market equilibrium.

2.66 The above discussion has focused on the short run situation. In the long run, if the price is fixed at a very profitable level, there will be an incentive for new producers to enter the market and for existing producers to increase capacity. Thus there is a long run tendency for excess demand to disappear. This process and its effects will be discussed in the next chapter. Here, the essential point is that giving firms responsibility for sales is not sufficient to create an incentive for intensive growth. A necessary precondition is elimination of excess demand which creates a seller's market.

3. ENTERPRISE RESPONSE, 1980-82

3.01 The reforms and policy measures described in Chapter 2 eliminated the most important constraints preventing CCWC's expansion of production. Adequate financial resources for investment were made available, mainly from enterprise retained profits and bank loans. CCWC was given greater freedom to obtain necessary material inputs directly from suppliers on the open market.[57/] Other required resources like land and production facilities could be arranged for by means of the associations and mergers CCWC was now allowed to become involved in.

3.02 At the same time it obtained greater access to resources, CCWC was given considerable authority to determine how and to what extent such resources should be used. In the early stages of reform implementation, CCWC had the ability to make strategic decisions as well as short-term plans on its own, with surprisingly little interference from higher-level authorities.

3.03 Finally, CCWC was given strong material incentives to increase production and profits. The new tax system tied enterprise discretionary funds (retained profits) closely to total earnings, which CCWC shared in proportionately. Though bonuses for individual workers in CCWC were not geared closely to individual or group performance, the link between retained profits and construction of workers' housing gave workers a stake in increased company profits. The authority to market part of its output directly may have provided CCWC with additional incentives.

The Expansion Phase

3.04 CCWC responded quickly to the new opportunities opened up by the reforms. It engaged in a highly ambitious investment program designed to triple annual production of clocks and increase watch production nearly tenfold. In order to finance this massive expansion of capacity, CCWC borrowed heavily - a total of nearly Y 27 million in 1980-82, with an additional

---

57/ Raw materials were the least important constraint for CCWC, because watches require relatively few scarce materials.

Y 4.5 million planned for 1983 (see Table 3.1). The magnitude of this borrowing can be gauged from the fact that government investment in developing watch production by CCWC in 1970-77 totalled only Y 17 million. Retained profits totalling Y 10.3 million were used for fixed investment in 1980-82. Major repair funds and depreciation funds also financed significant amounts of fixed investment.58/ Total fixed investment during 1980-82 amounted to Y 38.5 million, including Y 5 million which CCWC invested in associated enterprises. The radical changes in both the amount and the financing of CCWC's fixed investment are apparent in Table 3.2.

Table 3.1: FIXED INVESTMENT LOANS GRANTED TO CCWC 1980-83 /a

Type of loan	Total amount (Y million)			
	1980	1981	1982	1983 (planned)
People's Bank	3.25	3.25	10.0	2.0
Construction Bank	-	-	6.0	2.5
Bank of China	2.8/b	-	-	-
Local Government	1.47/c	-	-	-
Total	7.52	3.25	16.0	4.5

Total for 1980-82: Y 26.77 million

/a This refers to loans granted rather than actual investments financed by loans, which are in Table 3.2.
/b This was a foreign exchange loan of US$1 million.
/c Y 850,000 of this amount was subsequently changed into a grant.

3.05 CCWC made these large investments based on its own long-term plans. These plans were determined by the company's perception of market demand in the Southwest China region, but neglected to take into account national factors, particularly the growth of older, more efficient producers in places like Shanghai and Tianjin. In 1980 CCWC set a very ambitious goal to produce 1 million men's watches, 300,000 ladies' watches, and 2 million clocks annually by 1982. These targets were proposed by CCWC but were never approved by higher levels. In 1981 even higher long-term targets were set by CCWC, for production of 2 million men's watches, 1 million ladies' watches, and 2 million clocks annually by 1985. This set of targets also was never formally approved by higher-level authorities. But until the drastic change in the market situation in 1981-82, CCWC made large investments and obtained

---

58/ As part of the reforms CCWC was allowed to retain for its own use 70% of the basic depreciation fees generated by its fixed assets, compared to 40% previously.

Table 3.2: SOURCE OF FINANCING OF CCWC FIXED INVESTMENT /a
(Y million)

Year	Total fixed investment	State budget appropriations /b		Depreciation funds		Retained profits		Bank loans /c		Other /d	
		Amount	(%)	Amount	(%)	Amount	(%)	Amount	(%)	Amount	(%)
1975	3.19	3.19	100	-	-	-	-	-	-	-	-
1976	3.02	3.02	100	-	-	-	-	-	-	-	-
1977	4.81	4.81	100	-	-	-	-	-	-	-	-
1978	0.92	0.80	87.7	-	-	-	-	0.11	12.3	-	-
1979	2.56	0.08	3.3	2.08	81.3	-	-	-	-	0.39	15.4
1980	4.96	1.00	20.2	0.62	12.4	0.68	13.8	1.39	28.0	1.27	25.7
1981	8.55	1.96	22.9	0.25	3.0	-	-	4.30	50.3	2.04	23.8
1982	25.00	3.29	13.1	1.42	5.7	9.61	38.5	8.73	34.9	1.95	7.8
1975-78	11.94	11.83	99.1	-	-	-	-	0.11	0.9	-	-
1980-82	38.50	6.25	16.2	2.29	5.9	10.30	26.7	14.41	37.4	5.26	13.7

/a Refers to completed investment rather than appropriations or expenditures. Percentages may not add up exactly because of rounding.

/b Includes various subsidies from higher levels and funds for trial production of new products as well as budgetary capital construction and renewal investment appropriations.

/c Includes loans from the People's Bank of China, People's Construction Bank of China, and Bank of China.

/d Major repair funds and loans from the local government.

numerous bank loans on the basis of these plans. CCWC was able to do this because bank loans were approved on a project-by-project basis without consideration of the long-term comprehensive production plan. Investment financed by retained profits did not require higher-level approval until recently.

3.06 Another aspect of CCWC's response to the opportunities presented by reforms was the establishment of numerous joint ventures and associations with suppliers of components and watch assembly points. These were seen as enabling CCWC to expand production more rapidly than if it had set about acquiring the requisite land, facilities, labor, etc., directly. CCWC has invested a total of Y 5 million in joint ventures and associated enterprises.[59/] However, the investment in joint ventures and mergers has been less significant than their role in easing certain resource constraints and getting around administrative barriers. The most important benefit of these associations is probably the scope they provide CCWC for exercising tighter control over the whole production process for clocks and watches. Thus at the same time that CCWC was gaining greater discretionary authority vis-a-vis higher-level organizations as part of reforms, it was tightening up supervision of the numerous, hitherto only loosely related production units involved in various stages of the production process.

3.07 Another major feature of CCWC's response to reforms was its efforts to improve the material well-being of its employees. Substantial wage increases had been instituted as early as 1978 and continued through 1981, accompanied by rising bonuses. The average income of non-temporary employees increased by 87% between 1977 and 1981 (Table 3.3). Average collective welfare expenditures per employee doubled between 1978 and 1981. These sharp increases in worker incomes were mainly the result of national policies. But CCWC's profitability and consequent ability to pay for large bonuses and collective welfare expenditures made a significant difference. This is even more true of construction of workers' housing, financed entirely by CCWC's own funds after the implementation of reforms. The average value of nonproductive fixed assets (mainly housing) per employee soared from Y 707 in 1979 to Y 2,234 in 1982. Even so, only workers who joined CCWC in 1970 or earlier have been provided with apartments. Thus continued large investments will be required to satisfy the workers' need for housing. This means that for the foreseeable future many employees will have a strong interest in CCWC's profitability.

59/ This presumably does not include financial investment in and other forms of assistance to enterprises that were incorporated directly into CCWC.

Table 3.3: WAGES AND WELFARE BENEFITS
(Y)

Year	Average wage per regular employee /a	Average bonus per regular employee	Collective welfare expenditures per regular employee	Increase in non-productive fixed assets per regular employee /b
1975	543	-	-	-
1976	514	-	-	-
1977	509	-	-	-
1978	595	-	-	-
1979	755	164	72	-
1980	950	180	99	383
1981	950	134	144	578
1982	899	146	168	890

/a Including all bonuses, but not wages of temporary workers.
/b Refers to original value of fixed assets. The total value of nonproductive fixed assets per regular employee in 1977 was only Y 707. By 1982 the figure had reached Y 2,234.

3.08 In addition to allowing CCWC to engage in an ambitious long-term investment program, adjustment and reform policies eased many of the short-run constraints faced by the company. As a result output of both clocks and watches grew rapidly in 1980-81, as can be see from Table 3.4. 1981 watch output was 186% higher than in 1979, while clock production increased by 73% during the same period, starting from a much larger base. Production of watch components sold unassembled by CCWC rose by over 400% between 1979 and 1981.

Table 3.4: GROWTH OF OUTPUT 1979-82
(in %)

Year	Clocks (units)	Watches (units)	Watch components (Value at current prices)
1979	7.0	54.6	410.7
1980	42.8	79.0	-3.5
1981	21.0	59.6	435.9
1982	-55.3	10.5	11.9

3.09 Though greater reliance on the market mechanism was one of the key objectives of reforms, before 1981-82 the market appears to have only weakly constrained CCWC's activities. Excess demand for both clocks and watches was substantial at the outset [60/] and was stimulated by the rapid growth of personal incomes and, in the case of watches, moderate price reductions.[61/] CCWC took important measures to promote sales even during the early stages of reform implementation, but its viability and profitability did not depend on these. The enterprise perceived that it could sell virtually whatever it could produce in the short run.

3.10 In an environment where the constraint of market demand was relatively weak and the profit margin very high, CCWC's response took the form of rapid expansion in output, with little attention to improved quality or technology, as well as relatively slow development of new products and styles.[62/] Reductions in costs were small in view of the large increase in production (see pp. 55-58).

3.11 This rapid expansion of output, with little quality improvement or new product development, was probably the optimal strategy for CCWC to pursue as long as the market demand constraint was weak. It is a typical pattern that occurs in unreformed centrally planned economies when an industry or firm is given priority allocation of resources and is ordered or simply allowed to expand production as rapidly as possible.[63/] Did CCWC's actual response to the new situation in 1979-81 differ greatly from what it would have done in the absence of reforms but with priority allocation of resources necessary for

---

60/ Excess demand for watches can be inferred from the fact that in the prereform and early post-reform period CCWC's Shancheng brand watch was rationed. Purchasers had to present a ration coupon along with their money in order to buy a watch. Because of their lower price, clocks may have been even more in demand in rural areas than watches during the initial stages of reform implementation.

61/ These price cuts of Y 10 for a top-grade watch in 1980 and an additional Y 10 in 1982 had the effect of postponing the time when supply caught up with and surpassed market demand. However, the primary motivation, especially in the case of the 1980 price reduction, was probably to improve the real standard of living and lower the rate of inflation as measured by overall price indices for consumer goods.

62/ Of course the development of ladies' watches started during this period, and investments were made to improve the styling of clocks. In 1982 the changing situation imparted much greater urgency to these activities and stimulated development of other new and improved products.

63/ Even in the absence of strong financial incentives, firms in centrally planned economies (as well as bureaucratic organizations anywhere) exhibit a strong drive to expand. Profit maximizing firms in a market economy also tend to expand rapidly when faced with a seller's market, of course.

expansion? This interesting question is unanswerable but suggestive. Reforms may not have greatly affected CCWC's performance (though they obviously affected its behavior) until the market constraint became tight.

Market and Other Problems

3.12 By late 1981 market conditions for clocks and watches began to change - very dramatically for clocks and more gradually for watches. Demand for clocks actually fell due to saturation of the market. Watch demand was still growing but supply was quickly catching up. National production capacity was growing rapidly and rationing was lifted for many varieties. Watches were moving from a seller's to a buyer's market and were faced with the possibility of the same serious problem of oversupply as clocks.[64/]

3.13 This was entirely predictable. So long as firms (or their local government sponsors) have some autonomy and are responsive to profit signals, the existence of excess demand at a highly profitable fixed price will induce new firms to enter and existing firms to expand production. So long as the price remains fixed at a level above long run marginal cost, producers will continue to expand until supply exceeds demand. At this point, producers have several choices. They can cut prices in order to gain an advantage over their rivals and to increase the demand for their own product. If prices are allowed to fall, the market will balance at a new equilibrium price. Producers may also try to gain a competitive advantage by improving product quality or variety. This could shift the demand curve outward and increase total quantity demanded at the controlled price. If the demand curve does not shift far enough to clear the market at the controlled price, however, some producers will be unable to sell all their products and will either be forced to accumulate inventories or to cut production.

3.14 National planners could do one or a combination of three things under such conditions of excess supply: (1) lower the controlled price in order to increase demand and reduce the incentive for further expansion of supply; (2) restrict the growth of supply through administrative controls so that future demand and supply would be in closer balance at the controlled price; or (3) remove all controls and let the price fall to balance supply and demand.

3.15 In the case of watches, the authorities did a combination of (1) and (2). In late 1981, they imposed new 1985 production control figures for watch producers and forbade new investments which would increase supply beyond the control figure. CCWC's production quota for 1985 was set at 1.4 million watches, less than half the company's own proposed target of 3 million. This restriction was enforced through the project approval procedure, particularly

---

64/ Stocks of watches held by commercial departments doubled in 1980 and increased by a further 35% in 1981. Stocks were said to be above the "rational" level by 1.7 million watches, compared to production of 28.7 million in the same year. See State Economic Commission, Investigation and Research Section, op cit.

for bank loans. In April 1982 the authorities also reduced the minimum controlled price for most watches by Y 10. Neither of these actions was sufficient to prevent a continuing shift toward a buyer's market, however. Thus producers still had an incentive to try to cut price or improve quality and variety. Investments to improve quality and increase variety were encouraged.

3.16 Clocks are provincially rather than nationally controlled. In this case, the authorities (at least in Sichuan) took no action at all despite much more difficult market conditions. Producers were left to cope with the situation as best they could. Thus, for watches the authorities took a classic planned economy approach of controlling supply and supplemented this by lowering the regulated price. For clocks they used neither planning (options (1) and (2)) nor the market (option (3)) to correct the situation. Clock producers were left with the worst of both worlds: neither prices nor planning was used to regulate the market.

3.17 The collapse of the clock market was the most serious problem faced by CCWC. It was exacerbated because the company was slow to recognize that conditions had changed. The Commercial Department (CD) warned CCWC at the beginning of 1982 that the clock market had turned bad and urged the company not to try to achieve its production target of 1.15 million clocks. The CD was able to put pressure on CCWC to reduce production because a new reform in 1982 gave it authority to "purchase by selection" rather than by order. CCWC resisted production cutbacks and questioned the CD's evaluation of the market situation, but after a market survey confirmed the gloomy predictions of the CD, the company asked for a lower production target and cut production sharply beginning in mid-1982. Final output of clocks in 1982 was 540,000 (compared to 1.2 million in 1981) of which the CD bought only 220,000. Stocks of materials sharply increased, and CCWC was left with very high circulating capital costs. The worst problem facing the company was redundant labor which could not be laid off. Under the terms of a merger agreement with a commune in 1980, CCWC was in fact supposed to employ 390 commune workers in clock production by the end of 1982, in addition to 380 workers already employed. Although the company was able to negotiate an agreement which avoided taking on new workers, it was unable to dismiss any existing workers from either the commune or the company's own labor force.

3.18 Increasing competition in the watch market did not pose an immediate threat to CCWC, but the action of the authorities to prevent saturation and oversupply created additional problems to which CCWC had to respond. The new production limit left CCWC holding equipment which it could not use. Investment completed before the ceiling was imposed was unbalanced; in some lines CCWC had equipment for 3 million watches, while in others it did not have enough equipment to produce even 1.4 million. Worse, CCWC faced heavy debt repayment obligations for bank loans used to finance this equipment. The reduction in watch prices in April 1982 cut CCWC's profit margins. A further price reduction in January 1983 did not affect CCWC's own watches directly, but it lowered the price of Shanghai watches and thereby stiffened the competition faced by CCWC.

3.19 In addition to these market-related problems, at the end of 1981 CCWC suddenly developed a severe problem of quality control with its first grade (Shancheng brand) watches. CCWC was unable to meet the nationally prescribed quality standard of 88 marks for a sufficient number of Shancheng watches.[65/] This endangered 1982 bonuses and confirmation of the 1981 floating wage increases. Production of watches was reduced while the company tried to correct the problem.

3.20 The net result of all these difficulties was that in 1982 watch production increased by only 10%, clock production fell by 50%, gross output rose by only 3.9% (versus 66% per year in 1980 and 1981), total profits fell from Y 17 million to Y 11.5 million, and retained profits (after payment of taxes and repayment of bank loans) fell from Y 6.6 million to Y 2.3 million.

3.21 The quality control problem and the changes introduced by watch planning authorities simply forced CCWC to confront more abruptly the fundamental marketing problem which was bound to emerge. In the long term CCWC faces increasingly stiff competition from other watch producers, shrinking profit margins, the end of the easy days of unlimited production expansion, and most likely a permanent reduction in demand for clocks. However, while the company faces a declining market, it has been left with strong financial incentives. Its overall reaction was to move from emphasis on production and expansion of capacity to a focus on marketing and easing the sales constraint.

Response to problems

3.22 The problem of watch quality which emerged at the end of 1981 was essentially technical, but stemmed from apparent lack of quality control during CCWC's drive to expand production. The average quality of first-grade watches fell from 90.35 in 1980 to 88.31 in 1981.[66/] In January 1982 the average quality rating fell to 81.07, far below the required standard of 88. A large number of Shancheng brand watches failed to pass a shock absorption test due to an improper taper on an axle. This was caused by machine drift and was not detected because of faulty component testing equipment. Intensive effort and a great deal of time were required to locate and then correct the problem. By June quality had been improved to over 90 marks, but average quality for the year only exceeded 88 marks in December 1982, after all engineers and technicians had been mobilized to assist with production. During the course of the year quality control procedures were completely revamped, and in January 1983 three watch factories were merged into a single unit (the Number 1 Watch Factory) to improve technical standards. This essentially technical

---

65/ Marks are awarded for accuracy, shock resistance, and water resistance and then aggregated for a composite score. Although the standard is set nationally, CCWC conducts its own quality inspection. The CD does sample tests before taking delivery.

66/ The Shanghai Watch Factory attained a quality rating of 95.75 in 1981. The average national quality rating fell from 88.1 in 1980 to 84.7 in 1981 and then rose again to 90.4 in 1982. See "Brief Introduction of the Shanghai Watch Factory" and Statistical Yearbook of China, 1981 and 1982.

and organizational response was stimulated in large part by reforms linking bonuses and the floating wage to target fulfillment. Bonuses were not paid for two months; though these were made up in September, final confirmation of bonuses was not assured until the end of the year. 67/

3.23 The quality problem also stimulated an interesting economic response: CCWC used substandard components of the Shancheng watch to produce a new third-grade (Kunlun brand) watch. Development of the new watch was started in May 1982; batch production began in June and sales in July. By October full-scale production and sales of the Kunlun watch had been launched. Thus CCWC was able not only to recover from its production mistakes, but to turn its mistakes into a profit. The launching of Kunlun was part of a longer-term effort by CCWC to diversify production (see below), but the main impetus came from the problems and opportunities encountered in maintaining the quality of components.

3.24 Apart from the specific responses to the technical problem of watch quality, CCWC's response to the more general marketing and profitability problems can be grouped into five categories: manipulation of the rules, sales promotion, new product development, price reduction, and cost reduction.

Manipulation of Rules

3.25 CCWC tried to mitigate the impact of its marketing problems by manipulating the rules restricting its actions and affecting its incentives. Some of these efforts have been mentioned previously. When it became evident that CCWC would not be able to meet its clock production target, for example, it applied to remove clock production from the list of targets affecting bonus eligibility. Later in the year CCWC asked for lower targets for both clocks and watches for purposes of general evaluation. The municipal Light Industry Bureau (LIB) in every case almost immediately told CCWC to organize its production in accordance with the requests. The LIB accepted responsibility for possible rejection of the requests by provincial authorities, though this possibility was evidently considered very slight. In fact, revision of plan targets appears to be so commonplace in China that it may not make sense to describe such requests as trying to bend the rules.

3.26 Manipulation was much more clear-cut in another instance. In 1982 CCWC was exempted from the tax on all its fixed assets, not just the tax on newly-created assets (contrary to stipulated regulations described in Chapter 2), because the retained profits which were supposed to have been used for loan repayment had already been used for other purposes. This decision was made by the municipal Tax Bureau and confirmed by the municipal government official session. The municipal authorities appear to have acceded to CCWC's request for exemption because Chongqing Municipality was responsible for its own finances and had already met its annual revenue quota set by Sichuan Province.

67/ It is not clear why CCWC was able to pay any bonuses at all until the end of the year, since the quality standard is supposedly a threshold which must be passed before bonus payments are permitted.

3.27 In yet another instance, the local branch of the People's Bank of China (PBC) helped CCWC evade regulations on investment. In 1982 CCWC wanted to increase its investment in associated enterprises. According to regulations only retained profits could be used for this purpose, but CCWC's reduced retained profits were insufficient. The company therefore shipped component parts to the associated enterprises on credit and counted this transfer as its share of investment in the joint ventures. This showed up on the company's books as an increase in receivables, which were financed by a circulating capital loan from the PBC. Since this contravened regulations, however, the PBC charged a penalty rate of 50% (interest was 0.9% instead of the normal 0.6% per month) and asked CCWC to work out a schedule for repayment.

3.28 Attempts to evade restrictions on its autonomy were not limited to dealing with the company's new problems. CCWC managed to spend more than the stipulated share of retained profits on collective welfare plus bonuses during the entire period 1980-82, and it has taken advantage of opportunities to pay special bonuses from profits despite attempts to restrict such payments.[68/] But manipulation of the rules was more pronounced and reached new heights of ingenuity following the squeeze on profits and threat to workers' benefits in 1982.

3.29 One common thread running through all of CCWC's attempts to bend the rules to its own advantage is the willingness of municipal authorities to lend a hand. To what extent is CCWC given special treatment as a result either of its status as an experimental reformed enterprise or a currently-favored producer of consumer durables? Statements by the LIB and other municipal officials that the reforms should be given "a fair chance" and that the experiments in CCWC "should not be allowed to fail for lack of resources" suggest that CCWC has indeed been given preferential treatment. This raises questions about evaluation of reforms in CCWC and about the replicability of these reforms throughout the economy. If reforms only worked because of special treatment, they cannot be expected to work when applied on a larger scale, for it is impossible to provide preferential treatment for every firm. In

---

68/ In early 1983 CCWC was allowed to give a special bonus of Y 20 per worker following the visit of the Finance Minister. With restricted opportunities for expansion in the future, CCWC will have an even stronger incentive to divert retained profits designed for production development to bonuses and collective welfare. The implications of this for national policy are discussed in Chapter 4.

addition, mere participation in an experimental reform may give rise to the well-known "Hawthorne effect".[69/]

3.30 The extent or effect of preferential treatment should not be exaggerated, however. Some of the concessions extended to CCWC were costless and might be expected to be part of the normal leniency of local authorities toward their enterprises. More generally, it appears that much of CCWC's success in manipulating the sytem reflected widespread features of the Chinese incentive system: a "soft" budget constraint [70/] and a slack planning system. These features raise issues which will be explored in Chapter 4. Here it is sufficient to note that CCWC's attempts to manipulate the rules and the municipal authorities' acquiescence are perfectly normal and understandable in such a system. Moreover, while manipulation softened and delayed the impact of CCWC's market problems, the company was still obliged to take vigorous action to counter them.

Sales Promotion

3.31 Direct marketing was originally intended to provide CCWC with an additional incentive to expand output. (The main motive was to encourage greater responsiveness to consumer preferences by putting the producer in direct contact with consumers.) Under the changes introduced in 1980, the Commercial Department's second-level (provincial) wholesale station in Chongqing was obliged to buy 70% of CCWC's quota (or within plan) watch production and 80% of quota clock production, rather than the full 100% of output it had previously purchased. CCWC could sell the remainder of quota output and all above-quota output to anyone it chose, including lower-level wholesale stations in the CD system or even directly to consumers. Prices were controlled at all stages, but the change enabled CCWC to capture some of

---

69/ This refers to a famous experiment conducted in the 1920s in Western Electric's Hawthorne factory. New organizational methods produced spectacular increases in labor productivity. However, productivity declined again after the experiment had been running for some time. Moreover, other quite different organizational changes produced similar results. The eventual conclusion was that workers responded positively to any increase in attention, so that the very act of conducting an experiment regardless of content showed initially favorable but unsustainable results. See Fritz Roethlisberger and William Dickson, Management of the Worker: An Account of a Research Project Conducted by the Western Electric Company, (Cambridge, Mass: Harvard University Press, 1939).

70/ Kornai has argued strongly that the "soft" budget constraint is largely responsible for shortages in socialist economies. A soft budget constraint means that the enterprise is not held responsible for losses; bankruptcy would never be allowed and the state might even compensate on enterprise for changes in conditions which reduced its profits. See J. Kornai, "Resource-Constrained versus Demand-Constrained Systems", Econometrica, Vol. 47, No. 4 (July 1979), p. 801-19.

the commercial margins on its products: it could choose to make direct sales of particularly profitable products or to particularly lucrative markets and still sell any output it wanted (including above-quota output) to the CD, which was hungry for consumer durables.

3.32 The impact on CCWC was sharply reversed when excess supply developed. In a softening market, the CD can limit its purchases to the minimum required and, more significantly, has a much greater say on the variety of products it purchases, since variety must be mutually agreed upon in the purchase contract. Thus the CD adds to market pressure in forcing CCWC to produce a product mix more in line with consumer preferences. In the first quarter of 1983, the CD and CCWC agreed that the company would sell 220,000 of its total planned output of 250,000 watches to the CD, but there was marked disagreement about product mix. The CD wanted to purchase 120,000 Shancheng (first-grade), 20,000 Shanhua (second-grade) and 80,000 Kunlun (third-grade) watches, but the company wished to sell 160,000 Shancheng and 40,000 Kunlun to the CD. The company wanted to sell more first-grade watches to the CD because it has a higher production capacity for them, they earn a higher profit margin, and they are less popular in the market than the Kunlun watches. The bargaining power of the CD - and the influence of the market on product mix - was greatly enhanced by the introduction of selective procurement for clocks in 1982. This enables the CD to purchase only the total number and varieties it wishes (rather than contracting for production of an agreed number and product mix) and throws more of the risk of declining sales or changes in preferences onto the producer. Selective procurement has not yet been implemented for watches, but in practice the CD will be able to choose which varieties it wishes to purchase if an agreed product mix is not incorporated in the contract with CCWC.

3.33 Since CCWC cannot lower prices on its own authority below the fixed minimum, it has made strenuous efforts to promote sales. The company has increased its advertising, stepped up its efforts to sell clocks and watches to third-level wholesalers in Sichuan and second-level wholesalers in other provinces, and expanded its retail outlets. Generally speaking CCWC would not try to bypass the Chongqing second-level station if it could sell all it wanted to that station. CCWC makes the effort to sell to other wholesalers in order to expand total sales. Similarly, the main purpose of the retail outlets is not so much to obtain higher prices for clocks and watches sold directly to customers as to expand sales by providing service centers for cleaning and repair of Chongqing watches. CCWC subsidizes the retail outlets and repair centers (most of which are cooperatives) by providing cheap spare parts and a flat subsidy for repairs under warranty. The present warranty period is one year, but the company is considering increasing this to two years. CCWC's excellent service network is credited with enhancing its strong competitive position in Sichuan. Although parts for Chongqing and Shanghai watches are interchangeable, most customers do not know this and still prefer the local Chongqing watches because of convenient repair services. CCWC has also introduced several market surveys in connection with its new product development. These surveys have helped identify shortcomings in functions and design which are harming sales.71/

3.34 The most extraordinary sales promotion efforts have been undertaken by workers in the clock factory. As noted in Chapter 2, the company was unable to dismiss redundant clock workers and had only limited capacity to shift them to producing watch components. However, it placed groups of workers on study leave, at full basic pay but without bonus, and in 1983 introduced targets for the Clock Factory which provided for loss of up to 20% of basic wages if the Factory fails to break even.

3.35 In early 1983 the company also introduced three schemes involving sales by workers of the Clock Factory. In the first, a worker takes a voluntary long-term leave of absence to sell clocks on a contract basis. The worker buys clocks at 4% below the wholesale price and sells them at whatever price he can. Only 8 or 9 workers have thus far taken leave of absence to sell clocks full time. The second scheme is also voluntary. Factory workers are permitted to sell clocks in their spare time at 0.3-0.4% commission. About 800 workers are involved in this scheme. Because of the small commission, the main motivation for participating is the collective incentive linking sales and profitability to wages and bonuses. The third and most drastic scheme is involuntary. About 200 workers who have no production responsibilities are assigned to sell clocks within Chongqing Municipality. If they sell 50 clocks per month they get full salary and travel expenses. If they sell more than 50 clocks they receive a bonus. If they sell fewer, their salary is reduced and they receive no travel expenses. Although commune workers are not discriminated against, the workers who are forced to sell clocks are less skilled workers who are unable to contribute to production or new product development; these undoubtedly include a disproportionate number of commune workers.

3.36 About 10,000 clocks were sold through these three self-sales schemes in March 1983. They are intended to be only temporary measures lasting for about six months. It is remarkable that such measures could be introduced even temporarily. The third scheme, in particular, seems bound to reduce wages. For this reason, it is also an interesting indicator of overall labor market conditions in China. In the socialist countries of Eastern Europe, such a scheme would probably collapse because in the tight labor markets prevailing there, workers would find jobs in other factories. In China, it is doubtful whether workers will find alternative manufacturing employment or, in the case of commune workers, choose to go back to agriculture. Even the

---

71/ The surveys are also very revealing with respect to the tastes of potential growth markets. In a survey of upper middle school students, for example, CCWC found that boys particularly wanted a durable shock-resistant watch which can be worn while playing basketball. The girls wanted a cheap, stylish watch with a short life-span because they expected to be able to purchase another, more durable watch when they start working or to receive a watch as a present from their parents if they go to university.

reduced earnings from selling clocks will probably be higher than earnings in agriculture.

Development of New Products and Varieties

3.37 For the Clock Factory, new product development is intended to provide employment for redundant workers. In the case of watches, CCWC is mostly trying to find new varieties or to improve quality in order to enhance the company's long-term competitive position. Development of new watch varieties began before competition increased and CCWC's total production was limited, but these changes have boosted company efforts to produce new varieties. On the whole, the company has been more successful in diversifying watch production than in finding new products to replace clocks.

3.38 The value of clock output peaked at Y 10.9 million in 1981 and fell to Y 5.9 million in 1982. In 1983, the Clock Factory expects to produce about Y 4 million worth of clocks and Y 2 million worth of other products, mostly timers for fans and washing machines. One problem is that obvious lines of diversification, such as timers, are also being pursued by other clock factories.[72/]

3.39 Three measures have encouraged CCWC to develop new products. First, it still has fairly large retained profits, 60% of which are supposed to be used for production development. Since expansion of total production is blocked, the opportunity cost of using these funds for investment in new products, new varieties, or quality improvement is slight. It is also still relatively easy to obtain loans for these purposes. The second measure is a state-mandated new product development fund, amounting to 1-3% of total profits.[73/] CCWC spent Y 300,000 in 1982 and plans to spend Y 400,000 in 1983. Prior to 1982, new product development was financed largely by state grants. CCWC still receives a small amount of grants from the municipality (Y 35,000 for two projects in 1983), but most new product development is self-funded now. The third and probably most important measure is the remission of industrial-commercial tax for two years on approved new products. Approval is not automatic, but when granted it is a very potent incentive, since tax rates are 40% for watches and 25% for clocks. One deterrent to diversification into producer goods such as timers has been that the industrial-commercial tax rate

---

72/ In addition timers are components of consumer durables which themselves face market saturation.

73/ Different arrangements are mandated for other industries. In machine building, for example, the new product development fund is 3% of sales.

on such goods is only 5% - too low a margin for tax exemptions to help cover initial high production costs.[74/]

3.40 These financial incentives are augmented by a system of awards given by all levels of government for product excellence. CCWC has won municipal awards for its Kunlun watch, a timer for washing machines, and a clock used by students. It also received a first grade provincial prize for a new 17.2 mm ladies' watch. CCWC has never won a national prize for its products.[75/] The prizes do not carry monetary awards but are useful in establishing a company's reputation.[76/] CCWC has also established a system of bonuses for its research workers. Awards are given to research and design teams for completion of particular projects. The designer of the Kunlun watch, for example, received an award of Y 150.

3.41 CCWC has developed several new products in the past two years. It introduced a second-grade men's watch (the Shanhua brand) in 1981, along with a 20.5 mm ladies' watch. These were both market successes, but an attempt to introduce a digital watch in 1982 failed in the marketplace. In 1982 the company introduced its highly successful Kunlun watch and a new 17.2 mm ladies' watch. The latter was jointly developed with the Shanghai and Qingdao clock and watch companies. Each partner shared development tasks and expenditures and will produce identical watch mechanisms with different appearances. Attention has also been given to quality improvement. CCWC has just imported Swiss equipment worth S.Fr. 4 million to enable it to produce watch cases of different shapes. Finally, the company has 13 new products under development financed by its new product development fund: a men's calendar watch, an analog quartz watch with date and day, batch production of the 17.2 mm ladies' watch, sample production of the same watch with a date function added, a student's watch, 26.5 mm men's watch with comprehensive functions, a student clock, a clock with date and day, a quartz wall clock, a

---

74/ The Qingdao Forging Machinery Plant (QFMP) has been far less aggressive in developing new products than CCWC. QFMP appears to have been deterred from new product development both by the low tax rate (and consequent low value of a tax exemption) and low profit rate (return on capital) on machinery products. Stricter definition of new products may also have been a factor.

75/ National prizes for watches have been given to companies in Shanghai, Tianjin, and Xian. See "China's Clock and Watch Industry".

76/ Prizes can sometimes provide the occasion for the award of a bonus to workers. QFMP was allowed to award a bonus to all workers after receiving a national silver prize for one of its machines. The national product quality competition offers three prizes: the gold prize is given for products judged to be of top international standard, the silver prize indicates top domestic quality but is not up to the best international standard, and the copper prize is only slightly lower than the silver prize. See Peter Kwok, "Seven Current Chinese Management Cases", IBER Special Publications, 1981, p. 19.

timer for fans, a timer for washing machines, a musical toy, and a gold-plated watch case. All of the products other than watches will be produced by the Clock Factory.

3.42 It is difficult to assess the importance of funding mechanisms and financial incentives in new product development. The Shanhua watch was partially exempted from industrial-commercial tax (reduced to 15%) and the Kunlun watch received no exemption at all. These products use the same components (sorted by quality) as the Shancheng watch and needed no special incentives. However, CCWC received a full two-year tax exemption for both designs of ladies' watches, which would have been unprofitable without the tax exemption. In fact, the 20.5 mm ladies' watch will be phased out of production this year and may have been developed only in order to get a tax exemption. The incentives may encourage minor modifications of existing products and bogus new product development. For the most part, however, CCWC's development of new products and varieties seems to be prompted primarily by the need to meet stiffening market competition in the watch industry and to find new production opportunities for the Clock Factory. Financial incentives simply enhance the impact of these changes resulting from adjustment and reform.

Price Reductions

3.43 The change from a seller's to a buyer's market has generated strong pressures for price reductions, but producers are constrained from price competition by controls fixing minimum prices for all products. In spite of these controls, CCWC has found ways to reduce prices.

3.44 CCWC was granted permission by the provincial Price Commission in November 1982 to reduce prices on some of its stockpiled clocks. Reductions ranged from 18-40% but applied only to inventories, not to new production. In the first three months after the reduction CCWC was able to clear 100,000 clocks from inventory, mostly by retail sales. Even with these reductions, few additional clocks were purchased by wholesale stations. In effect, the reductions have come too late. The market for clocks is already saturated, there is great excess production capacity in the industry, and many producers will be forced to exit from clock production. Had price reductions been permitted earlier, expansion would have been curtailed and adjustment would have been more orderly.

3.45 In the case of watches, the planning authorities have tried to intervene in the market by restricting supply and reducing regulated prices. This has been only partially successful. The establishment of small watch factories not listed in the state plan has caused the State Economic Commission to conclude that "planning is out of control and production is developing unchecked."[77] It remains to be seen whether state production plans will prevail over the wishes of larger producers listed in the plan to

---

77/ State Economic Commission, Investigation and Research Section, op. cit., p.33.

increase production significantly. As a result, strong incentives for further price reductions still exist.

3.46 CCWC has been able to lower its prices in two ways. The first is the familiar one of evading existing regulations with the cooperation of the municipal authorities. Although the minimum price for a third-grade watch is Y 50, CCWC is selling its third-grade Kunlun watch for Y 45. The company applied to both the provincial and municipal Price Commissions for permission to do this. The municipal authorities approved the request but the provincial Price Commission has not replied. CCWC has therefore been selling these watches at Y 45 within Chongqing Municipality but at Y 50 in other areas.

3.47 The second method of evading price restrictions is disguised price reductions through changes in the product mix. Since all three brands of men's watches are made from the same components, CCWC has simply increased the proportion of Shanhua and Kunlun watches which it produces. In some instances, the company puts a second-grade face on watches which would qualify for first grade, while reserving only its highest quality watches for marketing under the Shancheng brand. In this way it effectively has upgraded the quality of all its watches.[78/] Shanghai and other companies have also engaged in this method of disguised price reduction/quality improvement. The extent to which CCWC can change its product mix is constrained by its profit target. If it produces too many lower-grade watches it will fail to meet its profit target and may be unable to pay bonuses. CCWC's response is to try to expand total output. Its state-set production target in 1983 is 900,000 watches, but the company has set an internal target of 1.2 million watches. If it can produce a larger number of watches, it will be able to shift its product mix toward lower grade (and lower profit) watches and thereby both meet its profit target and respond to consumer preferences.

3.48 The pressure for price reductions (and tax reductions or exemptions by local authorities) is so strong throughout the watch industry that Xue Muqiao, one of China's leading economists, has questioned whether planning targets can influence production without more realistic prices:

> "Because our price system is irrational... we cannot limit the production of goods in short supply. Under such a price structure, to carry out guidance planning would only lead to greater...imbalance as a result of which enterprises are encouraged to organize production in violation of the state plan. If prices are not adjusted, even directive plans cannot be realized... [High cost] watch producers reduce their prices, some to Y 50-60, some to Y 30-40, to compete with Shanghai watches. If we let

---

78/ The company's strategy is to maintain an excellent reputation for the Shancheng watch and use that reputation to promote sales of all Chongqing watches.

this situation develop, not even indicative planning can fully play its role, not to mention guidance planning."79/

Cost Reduction

3.49 Cost reduction is an obvious third stage of response to adjustment and reform. In conditions of excess demand, the first response of producers is naturally to expand output of existing products. As the market moves into excess supply, producers should respond by increasing variety and reducing price. The system has worked well and CCWC has responded as predicted through the first two stages, but there is no evidence that the company has made much effort to move to the third stage of cost reduction. Although CCWC has reduced its average cost of production of watches by nearly 27% from 1979 to 1982, this appears to have been entirely due to expansion in the scale of production rather than to special efforts to reduce costs.

3.50 One would expect substantial economies of scale in the Chinese watch industry because of the large number of "small but comprehensive" producers. The unit production costs of some important watch components decline substantially with mass production. Thus, while specialized assembly plants might be able to compete with large integrated producers, small integrated producers would be expected to have very high costs of production. This is confirmed in the 1980 cost and output data for the 29 largest Chinese watch factories, shown in Figure 3.1. The figure shows the scatter diagram of observations and the ordinary least squares regression line based on the observations. The regression equation estimating the log of costs as a function of the log of output indicates that for every doubling of output, the cost of production falls by 20.5%.80/

3.51 CCWC's production costs did not fall as fast during 1979-82 as would have been predicted by the regression equation for a firm which more than tripled its output. Table 3.5 shows that whereas CCWC's predicted and actual costs were equal in 1979 when it was producing 280,000 watches, the company's actual costs in 1982 were 7.5% above predicted costs at an output of over

---

79/ Xue Muqiao, "Theory of Economic System Reform - Several Issues for Further Discussion," Speech delivered in a conference on the theory of economic system reform, September 25, 1982, published in Economic Research, 1983 (8), p.5.

80/ The results are: $\log C = \underset{(.044)}{2.838} - \underset{(.036)}{0.332} (\log O)$,

where C = cost and O = output. Adjusted r2 = 0.76. The t values are 64.6 for the intercept and -9.4 for log O. Standard errors are shown in parentheses. Data are from State Economic Commission, Investigation and Research Section, Economic Investigations, No. 1 (October 1983), Tables 1 and 2, p. 36. The regression excludes the Nanjing Watch Factory and the three smallest factories in Table 2. The former produces only economy watches with few jewels and the latter appear to be non-integrated assembly plants.

FIGURE 3.1
THE RELATIONSHIP BETWEEN OUTPUT AND COST OF PRODUCTION FOR
29 CHINESE WATCH FACTORIES, 1980

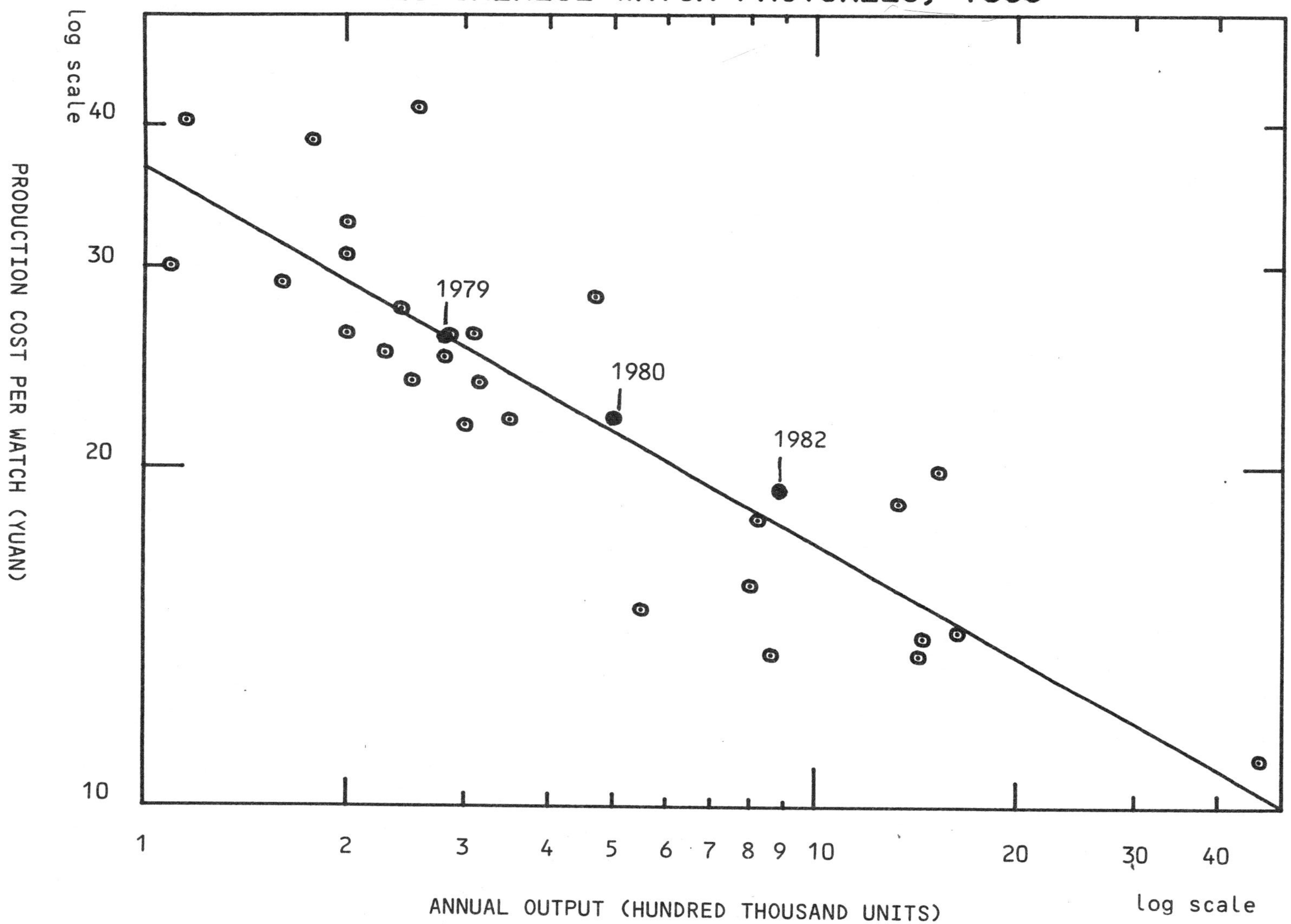

880,000 watches. In Figure 3.1 the three observations for CCWC are indicated by solid circles and dated (only 1980 is included in the regression). CCWC's failure to lower costs in line with output expansion shows up as a movement away from the regression line. The lag in CCWC's cost reduction should not be overemphasized. The divergence is not statistically significant and adjustment for inflation might change the results. Moreover, both costs and output may reflect managerial efficiency rather than being directly linked through economies of scale.[81/]

Table 3.5: PREDICTED AND ACTUAL WATCH PRODUCTION COSTS FOR CCWC (Y)

Year	Production	Predicted cost	Actual cost	Absolute difference	% difference
1979	280,000	26.06	26.06	0	0
1980	501,210	21.49	22.15	0.66	3.1
1982	883,923	17.80	19.14	1.34	7.5

Source: Predicted cost is from the regression equation. CCWC's costs for 1979 and 1982 are from Economic Management, 1983(9), p.24.

3.52 With all of these qualifications, however, the fact remains that CCWC's reductions in cost have been considerably smaller than normally associated with a large output expansion. In 1980, CCWC was the highest cost producer amongst eleven Chinese enterprises manufacturing 500,000 or more watches per year. By 1982 it was still next-to-highest cost producer (comparing CCWC's 1982 cost with the 1980 costs of others) despite an increase in output of over 75%. Thus it seems fair to interpret CCWC's cost reduction as only an incidental result of economies of scale. This is consistent with interview evidence suggesting that the company's management has only recently begun to pay attention to cost reduction. If the company is to continue to meet the challenge offered by reforms, cost reduction will have to be given much greater attention in future.

81/ This is clearly the case for the two largest producers, the Shanghai Watch Company (output 4.63 million) and the Tianjin Watch Company (output 1.63 million). The Tianjin Company has more fixed assets and nearly as many workers as Shanghai but produces only about one-third as many watches. Shanghai's higher efficiency is reflected in higher output and lower unit cost; lower costs are not caused by a larger scale plant, which is the usual interpretation of economies of scale. Ironically, Shanghai's actual cost is above the cost predicted for its scale of output while Tianjin's actual cost is below its predicted cost. One must be cautious, therefore, in interpreting the divergence from the regression line as an indication of inefficiency.

4. IMPLICATIONS OF CCWC's EXPERIENCE

4.01 Basing general conclusions about economic reforms in Chinese state-owned industry on only one or a few case studies is a difficult and risky task. The obvious danger is that the enterprises investigated are atypical or were provided special treatment during reform implementation, so their experience is radically different from that of other firms and moreover cannot be replicated. When observations are based on information from only a small number of enterprises, they may be unduly influenced by the particular circumstances and problems faced by the relatively few industries covered by the sample.

4.02 Despite these and other difficulties, this chapter will attempt to make some general statements about the present situation in Chinese state industry. Several factors ameliorate the problems arising from the single case study upon which the assessment is based. In the first place, material based on interviews conducted at a second enterprise, the Qingdao Forging Machinery Plant (QFMP), can be used where appropriate. Secondly, there is sufficient macroeconomic and sectoral information on Chinese industry to allow us to ascertain whether the experience of CCWC or QFMP differs radically from that of the industrial sector as a whole or that of the particular industries to which the two enterprises belong. Finally, the conclusions drawn here should be viewed as tentative ideas and hypotheses, which may be supported or refuted by evidence from subsequent case studies.

The Role of the Market

4.03 During the past several years the dominant influence on both of the enterprises studied has been the market, not directive plans promulgated by supervisory organizations. In the case of CCWC the most crucial reform measure may not have been the implementation of the tax system in 1980, but rather the end of guaranteed purchase by the commercial system of all of CCWC's output regardless of market demand. In the machine-building industry the change from unified purchases to allowing sales to be determined largely by market demand occurred earlier, and based on the experience of QFMP, the impact on enterprise behavior has also been strong. For both CCWC and QFMP, the effect has been to remove the buffer between the firm's own sales (and therefore its production decisions) and market demand.

4.04 Of course the sources of demand are quite different for producer goods and consumer goods. In the case of consumer durables like clocks and watches, demand is affected primarily by people's incomes and tastes and by commodity prices. Adjustment policies have stimulated demand by sharply increasing personal incomes in both urban and rural areas. Demand has been further increased by sharp price reductions in the case of stockpiled clocks and moderate ones in the case of watches.

4.05 Price is probably a much less important determinant of demand for differentiated producer goods like the specialized machinery made by QFMP. Central government investment plans are a key factor, as are the amount of financial resources available to and discretionary authority of local governments and user enterprises. Adjustment policies have sharply reduced demand for machinery from the former source. Indeed, this was an important factor in the decision to stop unified purchase of most machinery. On the other hand, reforms and fiscal decentralization have placed more funds in the hands of enterprises and local governments; the increase in demand from this source has partly counterbalanced the impact of the sharp cutbacks in state investment.[82/]

4.06 Annual and short-term plans for many enterprises appear to be based largely on assessments and forecasts of market conditions. Where enterprise plans or actual performance deviates from "control figures" sent down by higher-level authorities, the latter are invariably adjusted (often retroactively) to be consistent with the former. In addition to being flexible, directive plans appear to be quite slack: they can easily be overfulfilled under normal circumstances.

4.07 Market demand has also been important in influencing longer-term enterprise strategic decisions involving investment projects and development of new products and varieties. Government pricing policy has been a key factor, through its effect on demand as well as its effect on profitability. Government sectoral and subsectoral development policies, which determine budgetary investment grants and indicate priorities for bank loans financing fixed investment, also play a major role. Finally, the central government has sometimes intervened to prevent new investment in industries with excess capacity. Nevertheless, the degree of enterprise autonomy in strategic decision-making, including initiating projects and obtaining resources to implement them, has been surprisingly great. Since market forecasting and information gathering capacity in China is still generally weak, it is not surprising that enterprise evaluations of the market situation are often incorrect, especially when it comes to predicting long-term developments or assessing the nationwide (as opposed to the local) situation.

4.08 In the case of both CCWC and QFMP, reliance on the market mechanism has had certain benefits: improvement of quality and stricter quality control; alteration of product mix; development of new varieties in response to market demand; and various sales promotion activities. Response to the market has also been different in numerous respects. Differences in response can be attributed in part to varying circumstances of the two industries to which CCWC and QFMP belong. CCWC undertook a massive expansion in productive capacity, while QFMP did not. CCWC appears to have engaged in more extensive

---

82/ The change in the source of demand has greatly influenced the product mix demanded, as is illustrated by the fact that QFMP now sells a much higher proportion of small presses suitable for the light and textile industries.

sales promotion activities. It has also been much more active in developing new products.[83/]

4.09 In general, enterprises' responses to reforms enhancing the role of the market depend on a number of crucial, industry-specific variables: (1) producer prices in relation to production costs; (2) the overall market situation (excess supply or demand); (3) whether the output is a producer good or a consumer good; (4) whether or not the product is highly differentiated; (5) the level of technology required for production; (6) the market situation for the main material inputs; (7) the rate of obsolescence of products and correspondingly the degree of importance of development of new products; and (8) the rate of industrial-commercial tax on the product.

4.10 CCWC and QFMP are very similar in certain of these characteristics: both produce products with a reasonable profit margin (1); the market situations they face (2) are both characterized by excess supply; and both produce differentiated products (4). However, they differ in the other five aspects listed, which in large part explains the differences in response to the expanded role of the market mechanism. Where the product is differentiated, quality and/or new product development are crucial, prices are fixed and allow a comfortable profit margin, the market situation is characterized by excess supply or at least rough equilibrium, and raw materials are not a major constraint, it is reasonable to suppose that enterprises' response to the market will be beneficial. It is possible to envision other situations where such favorable results will not be attained.

Manipulation of the Rules

4.11 One of the main conclusions of this study is that financial incentive systems at the enterprise level, like the planning system in general, are weak and manipulable. Enterprises can change the "rules of the game" to their financial benefit, and almost every enterprise on one pretext or another is made into an exceptional case, entitled to special treatment. Thus in both CCWC and QFMP the amount of retained profits and/or workers' bonuses have on occasion increased or held even when enterprise performance as measured by total profits deteriorated significantly. Tax exemptions were freely given to CCWC on various pretexts, and in one case a Y 850,000 loan from the local government was changed into a grant. CCWC was able to get local authorities to lower the price of one of its products, while QFMP arranged a special price increase for its smaller presses. Much of the manipulability of enterprise financial incentive schemes stems from the weakness of the planning system. To the extent that rewards depend on fulfillment of directive plans set by supervisory organizations, they are only loosely

---

83/ To some extent this is just a question of definitions. For CCWC, ladies' watches (or even, apparently, a new variety of men's watches) are considered a new product, while for QFMP electrically-controlled small friction presses are considered an improved version of the same product rather than a new product.

related to actual performance, and there is a tendency toward upward drift in enterprise and individual rewards.

4.12 At the level of individual workers, there is somewhat stricter control from outside the enterprise. The total wage bill and the average level of bonuses is limited by labor and industrial departments and is monitored fairly closely by banks. However, enterprises have been able to get around these restrictions by increasing welfare benefits and constructing more workers' housing, using retained profits. Moreover, various special bonuses (above the limits) have been awarded in both enterprises studied, subject to approval on a case-by-case basis.84/

4.13 All in all, there is abundant evidence that in China the enterprise budget constraint remains "soft," despite the fact that the market constraint has become rather tight for many firms. No matter what the circumstances, it is virtually inconceivable that the Chinese Government would allow enterprises like CCWC and QFMP to go bankrupt. China and Yugoslavia may be the only socialist countries where many firms may be characterized simultaneously by a soft budget constraint and a "hard" market constraint.85/

4.14 The manipulability of the incentive environment and the soft budget constraint do have certain benefits. The system responds with considerable flexibility to adverse situations. In particular, measures are taken to maintain worker incomes in the face of a deterioration in enterprise performance, especially when it can be attributed to factors beyond the enterprise's control. Though this may seem unjustified, the alternatives of laying off workers or lowering incomes for all employees would most probably result in a decline in morale and productivity. This in turn would cause a further deterioration in enterprise performance, starting a vicious downward spiral.

4.15 The system has not, as one might have expected, distracted CCWC's attention from improving performance. Though some efforts have been made to distort the incentive system to benefit the enterprise and its employees, the very ease with which this could be done meant that it did not interfere greatly with attempts to improve quality, develop new products, etc.

4.16 The manipulability of the incentive environment does cause certain problems and raises important long-term issues. It may be one reason why efforts on the part of CCWC and QFMP to reduce costs appear to have been weak and largely unsuccessful so far. More important, the system is very unstable and unpredictable from the perspective of the enterprise. For many Chinese

---

84/ In QFMP bonuses were given out because the factory had received a silver medal in recognition of the quality of its product; more important, large bonuses were given out using funds provided QFMP by other factories for designing and producing specialized pieces of equipment.

85/ State enterprises in many nonsocialist countries operate under similar conditions.

enterprises the financial incentive system has been unstable anyway, with provisions changed nearly every year. For a firm like CCWC, however, the formal income tax system is fairly stable. In this case the weakness of the incentive environment reintroduces instability in disguised form. Also, by loosening the link between enterprise performance and enterprise and individual rewards, incentives at the margin are undoubtedly harmed.

4.17 More generally, tailoring incentive systems to the needs of each individual enterprise is not an appropriate pattern for comprehensive system reform. There will always be inequities and "objective circumstances" that impinge more on some enterprises than on others, but beyond a certain point the disadvantages of *ad hoc* corrections and tailor-made schemes far outweigh any supposed advantages due to improved equity. Indeed, at the worst extreme the manipulable environment degenerates into an administered system where formal rules mean little and each matter is decided on an ad hoc, case-by-case basis. This is probably no better than the prereform system, and may well be worse than a tightly planned, well-controlled system.

The Impact of the Unreformed Labor Allocation System

4.18 Labor allocation remains one of the most unreformed parts of China's state-owned industrial system. Binding quotas set by supervisory agencies determine enterprise employment. Workers are never laid off to economize on costs or because of poor market conditions, while on the other hand hiring of additional regular employees is a cumbersome and time-consuming process, often virtually impossible in the short run. Thus the labor system affects enterprise decisions both in an upturn and in a downturn.

4.19 For many enterprises, including CCWC during its expansion phase before 1982, the labor system restricts growth of employment. Enterprises with rapidly increasing output naturally desire to hire additional laborers. Moreover, enterprise decisionmakers may see additional wage payments as a benefit rather than a cost if they are maximizing income accruing to the enterprise and its employees rather than merely retained profits. The ability to hire sons and daughters of existing workers also provides a strong incentive to expand the labor force.

4.20 To ease or get around the perceived labor constraint, CCWC engaged in a number of activities, including associations and mergers with other enterprises and hiring of temporary workers, which were not subject to state quotas. In some cases other firms may buy large amounts of new equipment and use an overly capital-intensive production process as a result of the labor constraint. The artificially induced labor shortage can lead to hoarding of labor by enterprises, akin to hoarding of materials in short supply.

Enterprises may not need all of the workers they have, but they hold onto them and even strive to hire more labor in order to meet future contingencies.86/

4.21 The enterprise response to a downturn, such as that faced by CCWC in 1982, is just as important. Since it cannot and in any case probably does not want to lay off workers, a firm is forced to find ways to keep them occupied. One obvious way to do this is by dividing up tasks so that a given amount of work is spread out among more workers. In situations where new equipment or improved technology might have otherwise caused a sharp rise in labor productivity, the net result might be stagnant or only slowly rising productivity.

4.22 A second type of response is the channeling of excess labor into auxiliary activities, which often earn low returns. Provision of additional services to the other employees of the enterprise, utilization of waste materials generated in the production process, additional minor processing of the firm's output, even the involvement of some employees in retail commerce, are all examples of this type of activity. In some cases the private returns to the enterprise are substantial but the social returns may be zero or negative, e.g. when an enterprise uses its excess labor to perform operations which were previously undertaken by other firms.87/ Even if returns from this type of response to a deteriorating market situation are low, these actions are more beneficial than greater idleness on the job. The opportunity cost of the resources used is near zero; more important, the damaging effects of work-sharing on morale and work habits are avoided.

4.23 Inability to lay off workers may also deter a firm from undertaking risky new activities. If an expansion project fails, the enterprise risks not only having to write off a bad investment but also carrying a permanently

---

86/ The common perception outside China is that industrial enterprises are overstaffed. They frequently are in the sense that fewer workers could produce the same output with minimal reorganization of production and greater effort by remaining workers. However, workers have little incentive to increase effort, and unreformed enterprises have little incentive to reduce costs. Unreformed enterprises may have an objective function which makes them more expansionary than a profit maximizing firm would be. Carefully chosen reforms can affect incentives to use labor efficiently, however. Responsibility for sales plus the emergence of excess supply have made both CCWC and QFMP much less willing to expand employment now than in the past.

87/ Since CCWC is an industrial corporation with production largely integrated under its control and considerable responsibility for all production units, this option is largely unavailable to it. However, it can be hypothesized that when the market situation worsens, conflict among the various subunits over division of a diminishing pie becomes sharper, and that certain enterprises most loosely associated with CCWC suffer disproportionately as a result.

redundant labor force.[88/] As a result of its experience with the commune merger to provide a new site for the clock factory, CCWC will undoubtedly be much more averse to such risky, employment-expanding activities in the future. To the extent that this promotes more cautious analysis of projects it is beneficial, but it could also introduce a socially suboptimal degree of risk aversion.

4.24 The most interesting and strategically the most important response of a firm with a fixed labor force to deteriorating market conditions is diversification into new lines of products. This is illustrated most prominently by the effort to develop new products at the clock factory in the wake of the collapse of the market for clocks in 1982.[89/]

4.25 In many respects product diversification is beneficial. Instead of workers being laid off and then presumably at some later point being hired by other factories producing for markets where demand is expanding, firms look for such new opportunities themselves, while holding onto their labor force. Thus instead of search behavior by workers (for jobs) combined with entrepreneurial activities by capitalists, there is entrepreneurial behavior by firms seeking to keep their given work forces employed.[90/] Particularly if the government has explicit or implicit obligations to maintain the consumption levels of workers during the process of transition, diversification by firms may well be a less socially costly means of shifting economic activity in response to the changing structure of demand than laying off workers.

4.26 The relative benefits of diversification also depend on technical conditions: the degree of specialization of the firm's equipment, the level and types of skills in the workforce, the nature of the product previously made, and its degree of similarity to other products. If an enterprise diversifies into new product lines where it has a technical advantage and market demand is strong, the effect should be positive. But on the other hand if firms get into product lines which they are not really suited to and for which market demand is already less than supply, the effect is probably

---

88/ This depends on the scale of the innovation in relation to the scale of the firm. A large or rapidly growing enterprise will be less affected by this consideration than a small firm or an enterprise in a stagnant industry.

89/ Development of new product lines is a qualitatively different activity from production of new varieties or similar products to ease the demand constraint within a single market. Examples of the latter are CCWC's production of thinner, more stylish men's watches and of course the low-priced Kunlun brand. See Chapter 3 for a detailed discussion of new product development at CCWC.

90/ Search behavior by firms also occurs in market economies, of course, particularly among large Japanese firms with a tradition of providing lifetime employment to workers.

harmful. Much diversification in Chinese industry during the past few years has been of the latter type.91/

4.27 In the particular case of CCWC, the technical basis and skills are present. However, many of the products which CCWC is technically suited to diversify into are consumer durables (or parts of consumer durables) and other goods characterized by incipient or actual market saturation, due to a combination of high prices and entry by numerous other machinery producers trying to diversify.

Investment Financing

4.28 We have already seen that CCWC obtained significant discretionary authority in the area of investment decisionmaking as part of the reforms. It was also provided with financial resources to implement investment projects (in the form of retained profits and bank loans). These helped enable the company to expand rapidly in response to high demand for its products.

4.29 When the market constraint becomes tight, as it did in 1982 for CCWC, retained profits can no longer be used for expansion of capacity in the same line of products. Apparently CCWC stopped investing in expansion of clock production capacity of its own accord. Capacity-increasing investments for watches have been limited by a national policy decision to forestall market saturation. Whatever the mechanism, CCWC is now effectively prevented from undertaking major investments designed only to increase production capacity. Other consumer durables producers face a similar situation.

4.30 Enterprise discretionary funds that can no longer be used for capacity expansion may get diverted in the first instance to construction of workers' housing and provision of other workers' amenities. Funds may also be used for "intensive" investments, which do not increase output but result in improved technology, better quality, more attractive styling, etc. Some investments may rectify imbalances in the production process or allow internalization of activities previously done by other firms. There is also the possibility that some enterprise discretionary funds may be used simply to increase capital intensity: though the firm probably has excess labor, the opportunity cost of its funds (which may be earmarked for investment anyway) might be near zero, in which case it will pay to invest in capital-intensive technologies despite the labor surplus.92/ In some cases enterprise discretionary funds may be used to finance circulating capital needs.

4.31 However, there are limits to the above types of investment, both technical and externally imposed. On the other hand, simply leaving the funds in the enterprise's bank account renders them vulnerable to confiscation or

---

91/ A good example is the production of electric fans by numerous machinery building factories.

92/ Greater capital intensity may also reduce the amount of arduous work and be strongly desired on that ground.

freezing by administrative decree, or the only slightly more palatable alternative of involuntary purchases of Treasury Bonds.[93/] Thus enterprise discretionary funds may sooner or later get diverted to investments in diversification of product lines. This reinforces the impact of the labor allocation system discussed in the previous section.

4.32 CCWC is unusual in being engaged in a very profitable line of business while at the same time retaining a relatively high proportion (60%) of its profits. But there has been a rapid increase in the discretionary funds accruing to many other Chinese industrial enterprises as well. Thus the incentives to diversify as a means of employing idle discretionary funds may also be building up in other firms that are tightly constrained by market demand for their original line of products.

4.33 Contrary to the situation with labor, where there are significant costs in moving workers from firm to firm, an efficient financial intermediation system can transfer financial resources from one enterprise to another at lost cost. On the other hand, diversification by a single firm entails significant transition and development costs. In China mobility of funds through and within the banking system is quite limited. Firms generally prefer to use their funds in self-financed projects or investment in joint ventures rather than depositing them in banks, where they earn only nominal interest.

4.34 The preference of Chinese enterprises to use their retained profits for self-financed investment rather than allowing them to be reallocated through financial intermediaries is similar to patterns in market economies, where as much as 75% of investment expenditures is self-financed. This suggests that the benefits of an efficient financial intermediation system lie much more in the area of providing appropriate signals on the opportunity cost of capital than in directing financial resources from net savers to those whose investment requirements exceed internally available funds.

4.35 A number of measures can ameliorate the incipient problem of excessive liquidity leading to inefficient use of funds or inappropriate diversification. Output price reductions may simultaneously stimulate demand and decrease enterprise discretionary resources, attacking the problem from two angles. Reductions in profit retention rates would be another possibility. An increase in the industrial-commercial tax rate would accomplish the same purpose. Any of these actions would be resisted by the enterprises concerned.

93/ These are a new revenue-raising device instituted by the Chinese Government in 1981. Mandatory targets for Treasury Bond purchases are passed down through the administrative hierarchy to enterprises. CCWC was required to buy Y 400,000 worth of Treasury Bonds in 1981 and the same amount in 1982. QFMP purchased Y 100,000 worth in each year. The bonds carry a 4% annual interest rate and have a maturity of 5-10 years.

CCWC's Performance

4.36 The discussion so far in this chapter has focused on broader issues and problems, making some tentative observations on the way in which the Chinese economic system appears to function. It is appropriate to end this case study with a brief evaluation of CCWC's performance in the new environment created by economic reforms.

4.37 In response to the new opportunities presented by the reforms, CCWC has exhibited behavior that can only be described as "entrepreneurial". It has acted aggressively to increase capacity, output, and market share in the Southwest China region. Its pre-emptive investment strategy and extensive involvement in joint ventures and associations enabled it to become the largest of the six relative newcomers in the Chinese watch industry, even though the company's 1985 state-set output target is far below what it desired. Faced with an emerging market demand constraint in the case of watches and disastrous market saturation in the case of clocks, CCWC responded admirably. Quality improvement, disguised price reductions, development of new brands and more attractive styles, and aggressive sales promotion were the most important measures the company took to ease the market demand constraint for watches. The clock situation was much more serious, and to deal with it CCWC took more drastic measures. These included reducing prices sharply, requiring about 20% of the workforce to go out and sell clocks themselves in order to earn their pay, and aggressively pursuing direct commission sales to wholesale and retail commercial units. But the key long-term response is a desperate search for new lines of products, in recognition of the fact that clock production alone will probably never fully employ the labor force at the clock factory.

4.38 The quality of CCWC's response to reforms depended crucially on the market situation. CCWC took advantage of initial excess demand in the marketplace by pursuing extensive growth development. As the market constraint tightened, however, the company could no longer rely on output expansion and turned to an intensive growth pattern. This is of course much more difficult than simply increasing output, but at the same time it is in the end more socially beneficial. Measured performance (particularly growth of output and profits) does not fairly reflect the quality of CCWC's response. Measured performance in 1980-81 was spectacular but was achieved relatively easily. On the other hand, profits and other success indicators declined in 1982, just at the time when CCWC became fully engaged in its "intensive growth" response to a much more difficult external situation. The true test of CCWC's capabilities and response to reforms came in 1982, and the company did quite well in view of the circumstances.

4.39 Of course the weak incentive environment, slack planning system, and relatively loose administrative controls over CCWC's activities allowed the company to channel some of its energies into manipulating the system to its own benefit. However, this manipulation did not prevent CCWC from making the other, highly effective responses.

4.40 The one instance when central authorities and planners intervened directly and constrained CCWC's activities was the imposition of capacity limits on all Chinese watch producers in 1982. It is too early to tell whether this action will be entirely successful in preventing market saturation of the type witnessed in the clock industry, but it pushed forward the time when CCWC could no longer depend solely on growth of output to maintain or increase its profits. This episode shows that central planning of major industry-wide development and selective administrative intervention can play a positive role. However, in the long run such administrative controls will not be an adequate substitute for continued reductions in the price of watches to stimulate demand and eventually discourage further expansion of production capacity.

4.41 In terms of the future, based on its search for appropriate new products and responsiveness to market demand, CCWC's prospects would appear to be good. It will be squeezed by increasing market competition and continuing pressures to reduce watch prices. In its efforts to maintain profitability the company eventually will have to focus on cost reduction. Diversification appears to be essential for the clock production branch of CCWC, but it will not be easy and will almost certainly lead to new problems. In the more distant future, CCWC will probably have to make far-reaching choices on whether it will remain primarily a watch producer, even if this means shifting to electronic watches, or whether it is more appropriate to use its precision machinery and technical skills for other purposes.

4.42 The development of CCWC during the past few years presents a case study in the crucial shift from extensive to intensive growth, brought on by the enterprise's changing response to reform measures and, especially, market conditions. This transition is the primary goal of Chinese economic reforms. In this context the question of whether CCWC's success can be replicated throughout Chinese industry looms important. The enterprise unquestionably did get special help in various forms from different sources, due to its prominence in the reform experiments and its status as a producer of consumer durables. Even in the absence of overt aid, CCWC may have done better than it would have if it had not been in the limelight. These conditions cannot be duplicated in industry-wide reforms.

4.43 On the other hand, a key determinant of CCWC's success was its orientation toward market demand, in a situation where excess demand was rapidly eliminated and replaced by rough equilibrium or excess supply. This set of circumstances could be widely replicated, through a combination of market-oriented reforms and price changes. In fact, there is some evidence that in Chinese industry as a whole the market is gradually becoming more important as a resource allocation mechanism. All in all, the core of CCWC's experience and success would seem to be relevant for wider application, and to a certain extent can provide guidance for future reforms in Chinese industry.

MANAGEMENT REFORMS IN THE QINGDAO FORGING MACHINERY PLANT

Chen Jiyuan

Xu Lu

Tang Zongkun

Chen Lantong

Table of Contents

1. INTRODUCTION

1.01 The Qingdao Forging Machinery Plant is one of China's most important factories of its kind. It produces mainly twin-disc friction presses, with an annual output of 250-300 sets. However, the plant has had a somewhat varied history in terms of its output, management arrangements and financial success.

1.02 In 1951, the plant produced mainly ginning machines and water wheels, and had an annual output value of 127,000 yuan. In 1952, the state began to assign production tasks to the plant and appropriated funds from its budget for capital construction. With a view to improving management, the plant in that year abolished the "free supply" system under, which a worker's payment in basic goods was not affected by his contribution, and began to institute a financial management system and a system of distribution according to work.

1.03 During the First-Five-Year Plan period, in response to the call for local industries to serve major industries, agriculture, national defense and exports, the plant launched a program to identify and reward model workers, and introduced a system of piece-rate wages as an incentive for workers. Without any increase in funds, equipment or manpower, the plant increased its output and also added new products such as hand drills. By 1958, its total output value had reached 1.98 million yuan.

1.04 In 1958-60, when leftist policies were dominant, the plant pushed for high output and output value by rapidly expanding production. Its annual output and output value in these three years were more than twice as high as those in 1957, but most of the plant's products were of poor quality and expensive. Some of its products simply could not be used (in 1961, a single inspection found as much as 350,000 yuan worth of rejects).

1.05 After 1960, the plant began to manufacture twin-disc friction presses. From 1961-65, a program of readjustment and consolidation focused on devising rules and regulations that would lead to improvements in product quality. By 1963, the quality of the plant's products was higher than that of other enterprises. Annual output value, which was increasing annually but averaged less than one million yuan in 1961-63, reached more than two million yuan in 1964. Profits also increased significantly, from an average of 100,000 yuan per year in 1961-63 to 1.12 million yuan in 1966.

1.06 Despite some interference during the Cultural Revolution (1966-76), the plant was able to lay the foundation for future production by carrying out large-scale capital construction (it was relatively easy to obtain funds during this period because many enterprises had stopped production). By 1975, the plant's total output value had risen to 17.08 million yuan.

1.07 In 1977, the plant began a restructuring program with emphasis on improving product quality. The former level of management was restored and the quality of products improved until the plant again occupied top position in the industry. From the latter half of 1979, the plant started to implement further consolidation programs to improve its management.

1.08 More recently the plant has been affected by the Government's policies of readjustment and reform. Since 1980, the state has no longer worked out the plant's production plans, or taken responsibility for purchasing and selling its products, and for the supply of raw materials. Production quotas are now based on sales, an approach that combines planned regulation with responsiveness to market forces.

1.09 These developments have required the plant to make changes in its management practices and mode of operation. The plant has started to implement a system of independent profit and loss accounting for selected production shifts and groups. Labor norms have been established and an economic responsibility system based on "small collective piece-work awards" introduced. Control over inventories and equipment maintenance and use has been strengthened. The plant has also expanded repair services for customers. Finally, the plant has adopted new training programs for its workers. All of these changes have significantly improved the plant's performance.

1.10 The remainder of this report looks at the changes made so far, the success that has been achieved, and remaining issues or problem areas. Section 2 looks at the supervisory structure that has developed over the past 30 years, the types of problems that structure causes and a possible solution for simplifying supervision of the plant. Section 3 looks at the plant's readjustment to changes in the state's role in its production decisions and mentions areas that need further attention. Section 4 discusses the plant's economic performance since the changes have been made and suggests means for improvement. Section 5 looks at changes in the plant's labor and wage policies. Section 6 notes constraints to technological transformation and discusses work completed to improve old products and develop new ones, as well as constraints to further work in this area.

2. SUPERVISORY STRUCTURE

2.01 The Qingdao Forging Machinery Plant is a local state enterprise. It comes under the leadership of the Qingdao Machine-Building Bureau, which assigns its yearly production and financial plans and is responsible for evaluating its performance. Matters related to wages, the distribution of bonuses, and the recruitment, training and transfer of all staff (except cadres) must be approved by the Bureau; the Bureau then sends an aggregated report to the Municipal Labor Bureau. However, responsibility for appointing and removing factory-level and middle-level cadres and for Party organizations within the plant rests with the Party Committee of Jiaoxian County.

2.02 The Jiaoxian County Finance and Tax Bureau is entrusted by the Municipal Finance and Tax Bureau with collecting taxes from the plant and receiving the profits it hands over to the state. The branch office of the People's Bank of China in Jiaoxian County distributes and manages the plant's circulating funds, makes the loans it needs for production development, and supervises its use of funds.

2.03 The plant comes under the dual authority of the municipality and the county. The plant's output value target is included in the plan for Jiaoxian County, which is responsible for seeing that it is fulfilled. Other plan targets are set by the municipality.

2.04 The supply of materials to the plant is handled by the Ministry of Machine Building, the Shandong Machine-Building Bureau, the Qingdao Materials Bureau and Jiaoxian County. The central ministry is responsible for the distribution of raw materials needed to fulfill the production quota it assigns. However, for major raw materials (such as pig iron, steel products, nonferrous metal products, coke, fire-resistant materials and wood) needed to fulfill the production target assigned by the Municipal Machine-Building Bureau, the plant must apply directly to the Provincial Machine-Building Bureau; the Bureau then assigns a quota to the plant, on the basis of which purchase contracts are signed between the plant and the supplying units. The plant applies to the Qinqdao Materials Bureau for a coal quota, which is supplied by the Municipal Fuel Company. The Jiaoxian Commercial Bureau decides on the plant's quotas of gasoline, diesel oil and lubricating oil, which are then supplied by petrol supply stations under its control.

2.05 Few enterprises have such a complex supervisory structure (this is the only plant out of the 42 enterprises under the Qingdao Machine-Building Bureau with such a structure). In fact the supervisory structure of the Qingdao Forging Machinery Plant is the result of historical developments. The plant was originally an army field machinery repair center set up in 1946 in the liberated area. When it moved to Jiaoxian County (Shandong Province) in 1949, it was renamed Yinong Smithy. Since then, its supervisory body has changed 11 times. In 1951, it came under the jurisdiction of the Jiaozhou Prefectural Industrial Corporation and in 1960, the Qingdao Machine-Building Bureau (at that time it was renamed the Jiaoxian Forging Machinery Plant). From 1962-63, during the readjustment of the national economy, the plant came directly under the Shandong Machine-Building Bureau. In 1971-73, it came under Jiaoxian County. In other years, the plant's supervisory arrangements reflected the administrative organization of Jiaoxian County: at various times, it came under the Heavy Industry Bureau or the Machine-Building Bureau of Changwei prefecture or Qingdao municipality. The plant acquired its present name in 1981.

2.06 This kind of system causes many management problems for the county and the municipality. As discussed above, the Qingdao Machine-Building Bureau is in charge of the plant's production in terms of output and variety produced, but not in terms of output value, and it handles personnel matters for general staff but not the appointment and removal of cadres. It is therefore difficult for the Bureau to see that the plant is run efficiently. For example, the Bureau chose this plant as an experimental unit for restructuring in October 1982. After quickly completing preparation of a restructuring program, the Bureau held a meeting at the plant to discuss its conclusions. However, there have been no changes in the plant's management which reports to Jiaoxian County. Thus examination and approval of the restructuring proposal did not take place in March 1983 as originally foreseen.

2.07 As noted above, the Jiaoxian Party Committee is responsible for the factory's Party business and cadres. But the Committee and its agencies spend most of their time on agricultural affairs, and are not familiar with the plant's production and management. They therefore have no basis for making suggestions about the plant's organization. The county only pays attention to the plant's output value. It uses no objective criteria to assign an output value target, but simply calculates it on the basis of the output value quota of Jiaoxian County assigned by the Qingdao Planning Commission.

Issues and Recommendation

2.08 This complex supervisory structure culminates in serious difficulties in managing the plant itself and in optimizing production. Firstly, because of overlapping responsibilities, the quotas assigned often contradict each other, and the enterprise does not know which to follow. In 1982, the planned quota for output value assigned by the County was 19 million yuan; but the output value based on the quantity and product variety quotas assigned by the Municipal Machine-Building Bureau was 13 million yuan. With the assigned quantity and product variety quotas, the plant could not possibly fulfill the output value quota assigned by the county. Although the plant performed very well and made marked improvements in management--and hence was commended by the Municipal Bureau, the Provincial Bureau and the Ministry--it was criticized by Jiaoxian County for not fulfilling the county's output value quota.

2.09 Secondly, personnel management is divided between the Municipal Bureau, which is in charge of the plant's operations but not its cadres, and the county's Party Committee, which is in charge of the appointment and dismissal of professional and technical cadres. This system of personnel management is not conducive to the modernization drive. One reason for the delay in restructuring the plant's management is that the county's Party Committee is involved in too many other areas. But another reason is that the Committee is unfamiliar with the plant's production and management situation and therefore cannot evaluate the cadres affected by the proposed restructuring.

2.10 Thirdly, there is no single unit coordinating the plant's production, supply and sales; each activity is the responsibility of a different agency. Production targets are assigned by the municipality and the county. Responsibility for the supply of materials is shared by the central ministry, the province, the municipality and the county according to the category of goods and location of the materials supply agency. Domestic sales are handled mostly by the enterprise itself (and for some products by the municipality), while export sales are handled by the Ministry of Machine Building and the Provincial Export Corporation. With this management system, it is impossible to achieve a balance between production, supply and sales.

2.11 Fourthly, because the county's Party Committee is in charge of Party affairs and of the plant's cadres, it sometimes requests manpower, vehicles and materials from the plant for work in the county, and the plant's cadres usually have to accommodate these demands. In the past, the plant has assisted in combating drought, harvesting wheat, and repairing roads. The county is responsible for supplying petroleum products, electric power, paint and local building materials such as bricks, tiles, sand and stones, but there is no guarantee that the plant's needs will be met when these items are in short supply. (For instance, an electric power shortage is presently forcing the factory to stop work from 6:10 pm to 9 pm every day, no matter how urgently its output is needed.)

2.12 Fifthly, while the present complex management structure does cause problems, new difficulties have also been created in the past by frequent changes in the supervisory structure. Each new supervisory organization needed to become familiar with conditions in the plant while the plant adapted itself to its new leadership. Thus there has been little continuity and stability of leadership, and long-term planning for the plant's development has been severely hampered. Moreover, these frequent changes inevitably affect staff relations.

2.13 The problems described above clearly indicate that the present multi-headed leadership should not continue. Workers at all levels have strongly demanded that the plant should have only one supervisory body, irrespective of its level. The organizations concerned in Qingdao municipality and Jiaoxian county also agree that the present system, under which each organization has partial responsibility but can interfere with and delay the other's work, should definitely be changed.

2.14 In view of the modernization drive and in light of the composition of the plant's production and sales, it seems appropriate for the Qingdao Machine-Building Bureau to become the plant's supervisory body. The production technology used is complex; the plant's products are sold nationwide, with some exported; and the supply of major raw materials is handled directly by the provincial Machine-Building Bureau.

2.15 It would be inappropriate for the Jiaoxian County authorities to be in charge of such an enterprise for the following reasons: (a) they cannot rationally arrange the production of forging machinery products, or plan future developments in production; (b) they cannot guarantee the supply of major raw materials needed by the plant; and (c) they are unfamiliar with market changes and therefore cannot handle the sale of products. Their work focuses on agriculture, leaving little time for responsibilities in other areas. Moreover, county-level cadres lack modern scientific and technological knowledge, which would limit their ability to manage an industrial enterprise, especially a large enterprises in the modern industrial sector. Central authorities have decided, based on actual conditions in China, that key cities should gradually take over the leadership and management of industrial enterprise in their vicinity; management reform of this plant should also be in line with this policy.

2.16 However, once separate from the leadership of Jiaoxian County, the plant should still consider the county's interests. Development and expansion of the plant are dependent on the cooperation and support of relevant organizations in Jiaoxian County. The county supplies its electric power, local building materials and some other materials. The plant also needs the county's support in providing social services (education, medical care, etc.) for its staff and their families. Therefore, the plant must consider the economic benefits it can bestow on the county - perhaps handing over a portion of its income to the county as taxes or through other means. In this way, it would not only smooth the transition to management by municipal authorities, but would also promote good relations between the plant and relevant organizations in the county.

3. PLANNING AND MARKETING REFORMS

3.01 In 1979, when readjustment of the national economy was instituted, the Qingdao Forging Machinery Plant, like other enterprises in the machine-building industry, had underutilized capacity. For more than 20 years, the plant had received planned targets from the state and had its output centrally distributed, but this system ceased to exist.

3.02 Before economic readjustment was instituted, the state assigned to the plant annual directive plans with quotas for output, product variety, specifications, etc., while the relevant supervisory departments were responsible for production, the supply of materials, and marketing. The plant did not worry about products selling. As a result, for several decades the plant's top managers felt no pressure to make major changes in product quality and variety. After 1979, however, directive plans were replaced by indicative plans supplemented by market regulation: an enterprise's annual output, product variety and specifications were to be determined by the market and users' needs. While this new planning system has greater flexibility, it puts greater pressure on the plant. Thus the plant has had to change its past planning procedures and practices.

3.03 There are three main ways in which the present planning system differs from the past:

(a) Sales now determine output: the plant has to "find the rice for its pot," and has become involved in distribution as well as production.

(b) In the past, the plant simply carried out plans assigned by higher levels; now, it draws up the plans itself and then submits them to its supervisory agencies for approval.

(c) Production plans for the workshops are no longer based on assigned output quantities but are drawn up according to the dates of delivery to users. In the past, the plant could group production plans for the same product; now, its work plan is determined by users' needs, and often production of the same variety occurs several times during the year.

3.04 Marketing management has also changed. Before 1980, products were centrally allocated by the state, and the plant made deliveries according to the allocation list it received from its supervisory agencies. After 1980, the plant became responsible for the sale of its own products. It enters into supply and sales contracts with users, and makes deliveries according to contract provisions.

3.05 The staff of the plant went through a process of understanding the new situation. At first, they thought that as an important enterprise under the direct control of the First Ministry of Machine Building, their plant could easily get assignments, even during readjustment. Even when production was being reduced significantly in 1979, the plant still waited for the state to assign work, allocate materials, and sell the plant's products. The plant continued to send leading cadres to supervisory departments in the province, the municipality and the ministry to await assignments, but none were forthcoming. Marketing personnel were sent to many cities in different provinces with samples of their products, but very few orders were received. Help was sought from contacts in the State Materials Administration, in the form of a guarantee for the sale of enough of their products for the plant to survive; orders for 240 units of machinery were obtained in this way, which seemed to solve the problem. However, after only three months, these contacts found that too large a portion of their circulating fund was being tied up, and 80% of the orders were subsequently cancelled.

3.06 The plant's future course of action was discussed frequently. Reviewing the plant's development over the past 30 years or more - its growth from use of push-carts and belt-driven lathes to one of China's most important enterprises equipped with modern machinery - the staff agreed that they should try to overcome these difficulties resulting from the readjustment.

Reforms in Operations and Management

3.07 As a first step, reforms were instituted in the operation and management system. In the past, the planning and marketing functions were handled by two independent sections, although there were certain linkages in their activities. After 1980, the two sections were merged to adapt to the new situation in which production would be determined by sales volume and the market would act as a regulatory force. The new Planning and Marketing Section oversees the scheduling of production within the plant and keeps itself informed of the market situation, thus linking production and marketing. It represents an attempt to break away from the old management style in which planning was separated from marketing and production from end-users, and it is geared towards raising product quality, satisfying the needs of customers, and improving economic efficiency.

3.08 In its operations, the plant has begun to focus on socio-economic benefits, on improving quality and increasing variety of products, and on service to users. Before 1980, there were over 10 factories in China producing friction presses. After readjustment was instituted, many of these factories stopped production or switched to other items because their products did not meet the quality standards for friction presses. Only two factories - at Liaoyang and Qingdao - remained as state-approved forging machinery plants. The Qingdao plant now has 70% of the market. These developments have shown that users must have confidence in the quality of a product. In recent years, the plant has made great efforts to improve quality control. As a result, product quality has improved a great deal.[1/] Thus the plant has gained the confidence of consumers.

3.09 Moreover, the plant has changed its past attitude of caring only about the production of main machinery and neglecting the production of spare parts. In the past, the supply of spare parts often failed to meet demand, causing much difficulty for users. Now the plant tries harder to produce sufficient spare parts to meet users' needs.

3.10 The plant now also provides various customer services, such as giving technical training. It has organized a special seven-member team to assist users in equipment installation, trial runs and maintenance. For easy reference, it has set up product files for all the 2,759 presses produced by the plant in the past 20 years or so. Moreover, it conducts market surveys and forecasts and promotes sales, for example by setting up sales and service centers, visiting users, organizing user forums and introducing its products through advertisements and other forms of promotion.

Changing Product Design

3.11 The plant organized user service teams to visit more than 200 users in six industries (cutlery, spanner/plier hardware, bicycles, sewing machines, medical appliances, and fire-resistant materials) in 26 provinces, municipalities and autonomous regions. These teams promoted the plant's products and serviced machines and at the same time solicited comments and suggestions from customers. Many light industrial users commented that the presses were good, but were neither very efficient (they consumed a lot of energy), nor quite compatible with other machines involved in the production process, and thus they were not very versatile at a time of plant expansion. Users indicated that they would be willing to buy more if improvements were made in these areas. This process has enabled the plant's staff to identify broad areas where they could be of service. They also discovered that sales of their products had stagnated, not because the products were not needed, but because their design had not been changed for 30 years, and they no longer met users' needs.

3.12 In the past, presses were mainly used in heavy industries such as automobile and tractor manufacturing and lathe building. As readjustment of the national economy proceeded, the demand for presses decreased in heavy industry, but increased rapidly in light industry, which was growing fast. In 1980, sales to the spanner/plier and cutlery industries increased by 50% and those to the bicycle industry by 25%. Rural enterprises and the fire-resistant materials industry also began to purchase presses. Thus having different consumers of the plant's products has also changed product requirements. This

---

1/ For example, the 300T press won the state silver medal, the 160T press has met the "high-quality" product standard set by the province and the Ministry, and all other types of presses were raised to a higher quality grade.

new situation has forced the plant to change the circulation of its production and its product designs as described below.

3.13 First the plant has geared its R&D and production toward user needs. The plant learned from market surveys that the demand for presses would mainly come from the spanner/plier industry (60%), with smaller amounts for the cutlery industry (5%), the medical appliances industry (2%), the bicycle and tractor industries (10%), the fire-resistant materials industry (3%), and other industries (20%). As noted, the composition of demand is changing and demand for light presses is increasing. For example, China's cutlery industry is too poorly equipped to satisfy the requirements of international markets, and urgently needs to replace its outdated equipment in order to expand production capacity. The plant therefore organized technical teams to design and manufacture, specifically for the cutlery industry, a 160-TC twin-disc friction press, which can be used for cold pressing and precision forging of tableware, and which can raise efficiency three to five times. In addition, the plant also designed and manufactured, for a thermos factory, a compact and efficient 63T extension punch with a long stroke; and for the bicycle industry, the plant conducted research on and produced a 630T automatic, multi-position, cold extrusion press. In 1981 alone, the plant succeeded in developing 12 new products, which made up 70% of all product varieties manufactured during the year. These new products have proved popular and many orders for them have been placed.

3.14 Secondly, the plant has organized technical teams to tackle key production problems and is expanding its range of products. Experience with letting sales determine output has shown that if the plant is to get enough work to support itself, it must explore all possible channels, taking on new projects within its capacity while continuing to produce presses.

3.15 Thirdly, to foster the technical transformation of light industry, the plant has changed its past practice of supplying only single pieces of machinery and has started to supply sets of equipment for complete production processes. The plant has obtained contracts from two factories to build machinery for complete production lines, including the design and manufacture of equipment, its installation and trial runs. One of these factories is the new Suigang Hardware Tools Plant in Panyu County in Guangdong, financed by overseas Chinese, which plans to build three new production lines for tableware with an annual capacity of one million dozens, requiring 60 sets of forging equipment. The other factory is the Shanghai Medical Appliances Plant, which invested 1.6 million yuan in 1982 to build a new production line.

3.16 Fourthly, the plant has put emphasis on the potential market and on technical development. While modifying and improving existing products, the plant has not neglected its long-term development and is making a great effort to develop new product varieties. Because it is driven by friction, the twin-disc friction press, the plant's main product, consumes too much energy, is inefficient, and has too low a stroke frequency. The plant therefore considered design of a new drive mechanism an important item in its technical development program. In the past year or so, the plant has organized technical teams to research and develop a new spiral press. So far, it has designed and manufactured a 10T two-way spiral press, a 100T high-energy press and a 160T high efficiency, energy-saving press. These three new products, which are compact, light-weight, versatile, highly efficient and energy-saving, mark an important breakthrough in the drive mechanism.

3.17 These moves have enabled the plant to raise product quality and expand sales, increasing both output value and profits. Because the plant has had to seek its own markets and customers, and sell its products on their merits, there has been much better coordination between production and demand. Products have been basically suited to the market in terms of variety and quality. Orders were placed in 1982 (some for delivery in 1983) for a record 335 units of machinery (36% more than in 1981), and orders for 1983 have again exceeded capacity. There has been no new stock-piling. The plant's inventory of finished products--valued at 879,000 yuan in 1981 and 904,000 yuan in 1982--has remained within the approved quota (it was as high as 2,874,000 yuan in 1977 and 2,003,000 yuan in 1980).

4. IMPROVING ECONOMIC PERFORMANCE

4.01 During the past four years of national economic readjustment, the Qingdao Forging Machinery Plant has implemented the policy of readjustment, reform, consolidation and improvement laid down by the Party Central Committee. It has overcome difficulties and managed to develop itself in the course of readjustment. In the past four years, the plant sought new customers and opened up new markets, getting sufficient orders to maintain normal production. The plant's annual output of presses, which totaled 203 sets in 1978, dropped to 199 in 1979 and 176 in 1980, but went up again to 199 in 1981 and reached a record 238 in 1982. The plant accumulated a surplus and turned over profits to the state every year. From 1979 to 1982, it remitted an average of 2,649,400 yuan to the state each year, 742,900 yuan as taxes and 1,906,500 yuan as profits. In the same period, the plant was also upgrading old products and developing new ones, thus improving the quality of its output. Moreover, it exported 13 presses during this period.

4.02 These are considerable achievements. The plant had to reorient its production, expand its range of products and improve their quality, and strengthen its technical services. But most important, the plant conducted experiments in system reform, making adjustments in the relationship between the state, the enterprise and its staff, expanding the decision-making power of the enterprise in management and operations, and linking the economic responsibility of the enterprise to its economic performance and benefits. These reforms improved production incentives. In 1979, the plant was a pilot enterprise in the reform to expand enterprises' decision-making power, and in 1981 it was an experimental unit in promoting the economic responsibility system in industrial production. The plant has made progress in both experimental programs.

Financial System Reforms

4.03 The six major reforms carried out or being implemented in the plant's financial system, and the problems encountered, are described below.

Firstly, apart from contributions to the plant director's fund (equivalent to 5% of total wages) and the collective welfare fund (equivalent to 11% of total wages) in accordance with state regulations, the plant has implemented various profit retention schemes. Profits retained by the plant were as follows:

1979	310,300 yuan
1980	80,800 yuan
1981	242,500 yuan
1982	124,000 yuan
Total	748,600 yuan

4.04 Secondly, in 1980, the quota for total working capital approved by the financial department and the People's Bank for the plant was 9,634,000 yuan. Starting from that year, the plant has had to borrow its working capital from the People's Bank, except for 4,305,000 yuan, which was originally allocated by the state (from local resources). By the end of 1982, loans obtained by the plant totaled 11,417,000 yuan, of which 5,329,000 yuan was within the fixed quota for working capital, 3,880,000 yuan was above the fixed quota, 1,591,000 yuan was above the total quota, and 617,000 yuan was for settling accounts.[2/] Starting from 1980, the enterprise could also apply to the bank for medium- and short-term loans for equipment renovation.

4.05 Thirdly, since 1979, the plant has been allowed to retain only 40% of the depreciation fund, drawn at the rate of 4.6 %. Of the remaining 60%, 30% is handed over to the state, 20% to the province and 10% to the municipality. Before 1979, the plant had been able to retain 60% in some years and 50% in others. Nevertheless, the plant's fixed assets have increased every year since 1979. The year-end gross value of the plant's fixed assets were as follows:

1978	16,080,400 yuan
1979	17,523,600 yuan
1980	19,253,400 yuan
1981	20,626,700 yuan
1982	20,890,000 yuan

The value of fixed assets in 1982 was 129.9% of that in 1978.

4.06 Fourthly, the plant has established a three-level economic accounting system for the administrative and managerial offices, the workshops, and the shifts and work groups. In 1982, the plant instituted an independent accounting system for its workshops known as the "five quotas," "three guarantees," and "three evaluation criteria" (see paras. 5.14-16). Units and individuals with outstanding performance or contributions (i.e., achieving 50% or more above the quotas for output, quality and profits) would be rewarded

---

2/ The monthly interest rate is 0.21% for both the capital allocated by the state and bank loans within the fixed quota, 0.6% for bank loans above the fixed quota, 0.78% for loans above the total quota, and 0.6% for loans to settle accounts.

e.g. through additional bonuses. Those who failed to fulfill the quotas would receive no bonus for the evaluation period and might even have up to 20% of their basic wages deducted. In this way, the plant has developed a responsibility system whereby the economic responsibilities of the workshop are linked to its performance and benefits.

4.07 In the same year, the plant also implemented independent accounting systems for its administrative and technical offices, requiring separate accounts for management expenses, special funds, and welfare expenses, as well as for working capital. Moreover, work groups with appropriate conditions (at present about 40% of the total) are now treated as first-level accounting units and required to account independently for their own profits and losses. Work groups not yet ready for this system have separate accounting of such major indicators as output, quality, and consumption of inputs.

4.08 In this way, the economic and technical quotas of the plant have been subdivided into smaller quotas at every level and assigned under the responsibility system for each office, workshop, work group and individual worker (or job). Performance is regularly evaluated against these quotas and linked with a system of rewards and penalities. These measures have to a certain extent succeeded in rewarding those who work well and penalizing those who do not, thus creating work incentives for the plant's various units and individual staff members.

4.09 The effect of these reforms has been especially remarkable since the second half of 1982. Learning from the experience of the Capital Iron and Steel Corporation, the plant emphasized the rationalization of management, production and technical organization, and made further improvements in the various accounting and economic responsibility systems. As a result, the profits of all nine workshops in the plant increased from 46,000 yuan in the first half of 1982 to 113,000 yuan in the second half of the year (an increase of 145.6%), while the production cost of four major products dropped by 1.7%-8.1%. In 1982, the turnover of working capital took 74 days less than in 1981, and the plant's total profit was 37% above the planned figure.

4.10 Fifthly, for staff in the production workshops, the plant was implemented a piece-rate bonus system for the work group ("small collective") for work above the fixed quota. For staff in supporting departments and offices, a system of time-rate bonuses was introduced. For the plant as a whole, total piece-rate bonuses for above-quota work should not exceed 25% of total basic wages for the year, or three times the average monthly wage; the bonus fund under the time rate wage system should not exceed 12% of total basic wages, or 1.5 times the average monthly wage. Thus the total amount of bonuses is limited, but the amount of bonuses given to each workshop or worker varies and has no limit.

4.11 Finally, the plant has been allowed to continue the practice of including in production cost all expenses incurred during the year on research and trial production in the process of modifying and improving existing products. However, it cannot raise the ex-factory price of the modified products, no matter how much their design, performance, quality or cost effectiveness have been improved.

4.12 Progress over the past few years shows that the plant has taken rather small steps towards reform. The changes implemented have not changed the basic principle of "everyone eating out of a common pot." The plant has only limited funds for bonuses, so that the difference between the bonuses individuals receive is very small. As a result, bonuses have in reality become additional wages, and the plant has not been able to eliminate the basic egalitarianism in distribution. In terms of its financial relationship to the state, the plant still follows the old system of paying an industrial and commercial tax and handing over profits. Further reforms are needed which take account of actual conditions and the need for state revenue to increase.

Issues in Poor Economic Performance

4.13 The Qingdao Forging Machinery Plant has improved its economic performance to some extent because of its efforts to improve management over the past few years. However, despite the plant's success in matching production to demand (see para. 3.17), its economic performance is still poor. This is evidenced by its excessive use of capital (including fixed assets and working capital). Fixed assets and working capital used per 10,000 yuan of gross or net industrial output value have been increasing annually, as shown in the following table. The increase between 1978 and 1982 was about 25%.

	1978	1979	1980	1981	1982
	(thousand yuan)				
Year-end gross value of fixed assets	16,080	17,524	19,253	20,627	20,890
Year-end total working capital a/	17,534	18,017	17,485	15,535	17,628
Gross industrial output value (in 1970 prices)	18,903	21,093	20,884	16,555	17,357
Net industrial output value (in current prices)	4,745	5,280	5,234	4,428	4,353
Total capital used per 10,000 yuan of gross output value /b	179	168	176	218	222
Total capital used per 10,000 yuan of net output value /b	708	673	702	817	885

/a The year-end total working capital is calculated on the basis of the quantitative data (Appendix B) provided by the plant, as follows: No. 14 (year-end within quota working capital) + No. 15 (year-end above quota working capital) + No. 16 (year-end accounts receivable less year-end accounts payable).

/b Total capital used per 10,000 yuan of output value is calculated by dividing the sum of the year-end gross value of fixed assets and the year-end total working capital by the gross industrial output value or net industrial output value of the same year.

4.14 Another indicator of the plant's poor economic performance is the decrease in the amount of taxes and profits turned over to the state per hundred yuan of output, as shown in the following table. Total profits and taxes as a percentage of output value were lower in 1979-82 than in 1975-78. In 1979-82, the percentage declined every year until 1982, when it started to rise again, but it was still lower than the average for the four-year period.

Items	1975-78 (4 yrs)	1979-82 (4 yrs)	1979	1980	1981	1982
	(thousand yuan)					
Gross industrial output value	83,178	75,888	21,093	20,884	16,555	17,357
Profits turned over to the state	9,644	7,626	919	722	529	801
Taxes turned over to the state	2,926	2,972	2,714	2,561	968	1,383
Total taxes and profits handed over	12,569	10,598	3,633	3,283	1,497	2,185
Total profits and taxes handed over as percentage of output value (%)	15.11	13.96	17.22	15.72	9.04	12.59
Average annual total taxes and profits turned over to the state	3,142	2,649	3,633	3,283	1,497	2,185

4.15 There are several reasons why the plant's profitability has declined. First, the plant is incurring significant costs by continuing to carry unsaleable goods on its books and by using working capital far above its quota. The plant still has a huge inventory of unwanted products left over from the period when it pushed for high output value irrespective of customer demand. An audit of fixed assets in 1980 revealed 7 million yuan of such products, half of which were reported as worthless; even now, products worth 2.2 million yuan are still excluded from the account and are thus subject to interest as material in stock. Also after the audit, 1.5 million yuan of finished and semi-finished products included as goods in process and in the reserve fund had to be discounted or scrapped. More than half of these products had little use value,[3/] and some had to be sold at reduced prices. Because of poor management, the total amount of working capital used by the

3/ Among them were a double housing planer manufactured by the plant itself valued at 500,000 yuan; 50,000 yuan of unsaleable, poor-quality presses for manufacturing tableware; 400,000 yuan of new products that were unsuccessfully trial-produced; and unusable purchases, such as steel bars, worth many thousands of yuan.

plant at the end of 1982 reached 17.63 million yuan which was 7.99 million yuan above the approved quota. To improve the management of working capital, the state now charges enterprises fees or interest on the capital they use. At present, the plant has to pay over 100,000 yuan in charges to the state and over 600,000 yuan of interest to the bank each year. The increase in interest payments has raised the plant's production cost and correspondingly reduced the amount of profits turned over to the state.

4.16 Secondly, the prices of some of the plant's major products have been reduced. Since 1979, the price of the J53-630B press was reduced from 200,000 yuan to 180,000 yuan per set, and the price of the Y83-400 baling press for metal filings was reduced from 94,000 yuan to 80,000 yuan.

4.17 Thirdly, because of the economic readjustment, the demand for heavy presses has not increased, while the need for smaller presses used in light industry, brick making, technical transformation, and commune and brigade enterprises has increased substantially. This has led to fundamental changes in the plant's product mix. The output of high-priced, profitable, large presses has been reduced, while that of cheaper, less profitable small presses has increased. Thus total profits and taxes as a percentage of output value have declined. This occurs because the plant has no right to set its own prices. For example, the plant has lost money in producing the J53-160B press, which was priced at 16,000 yuan. In the interests of the enterprise, the provincial Machine-Building Bureau has approved a temporary price of 20,000 yuan starting in 1983. Another example was the J53-300B press, whose design and quality were improved, but as a result its production cost went up and profits on sales of the press declined, since the plant is not allowed to raise its ex-factory price. A third example is the improved J53-400A press, which is sold at 60,000 yuan and for which the plant loses 10,000 yuan per set. In addition, the plant loses money in most of its technical cooperation projects with other units. Therefore, the plant has suggested that the relevant departments should make reasonable adjustments to the structure of prices of some old products, the prices of improved products and the prices charged for technical cooperation with other factories.

4.18 Fourthly, because state allocations of fuel and raw materials to the plant have decreased in the last few years, the plant has had to purchase much larger quantities in the market at prices much higher than the state allocated price. Moreover, the prices of materials allocated by the state have also gone up slightly.[4/] Thus production costs have been rising rapidly. The product cost structure of the plant is made up of six main items: raw materials, fuel, power, wages, overhead expenses for the workshops and overhead expenses for the enterprise. In 1982, the total cost of products sold was 15.11 million yuan. Of this total, about 6 million yuan (or 40%) was for

---

4/ For example, the price of a ton of coke delivered to the factory has increased from 90 yuan to 200 yuan; one cubic meter of timber costing 160 yuan at the state allocated price is now sold in the market at 600 yuan; and one ton of tin, which used to cost only 9,000 yuan has a negotiated price of 29,000 yuan.

power, wages and overhead expenses for workshops and the enterprise, which do not vary much each year (the increase in interest payments mentioned in para. 4.15 could probably be offset by savings in other overhead expenses). The other 60% of the total cost was for raw materials and fuel, which were greatly affected by price increases.[5/] As a result, it was difficult to keep total cost within the planned targets, and profitability inevitably declined.

5. THE LABOR AND WAGE SYSTEM

5.01 In general, the labor, wage and bonus systems in the Qingdao Forging Machinery Plant follow state regulations. The required cadres and technical staff are assigned by the state; ordinary workers are recruited and allocated by the labor departments. The plant is not allowed to hire workers on its own, nor can it fire workers unless they violate the criminal codes or laws of the state. The plant follows the uniform wage scale set by the state for the industry. Collective welfare and labor insurance are levied at national rates set through state regulations. No factory can promote its workers or increase their wages without a directive from the State Council. Because wages are generally low and the living standard is not high, bonuses are usually given to about 99 per cent of workers. As noted above, the amount of bonuses is limited and the difference between individual bonuses is very small. Thus the bonus system plays a limited role in rewarding diligent workers and punishing lazy workers.

Staff Composition

5.02 At the end of January 1983, the plant had 1,662 staff on its payroll. Of these, 1,279 were staff and workers under the state ownership system, 299 were workers under the collective ownership system, 37 were contract workers and 47 were peasant workers. The staff breaks down into 1,264 workers (76%); 91 engineers and technical personnel (5.5%), of whom 13 were engineers, 18 were assistant engineers and 7 were technicians; 193 managerial and administrative personnel (11.6%); 104 service personnel (6.3%); and 10 other categories of personnel (0.6%), including those on long-term sick leave or study leave.

5.03 Some explanation is needed of the circumstances that led to a state enterprise employing workers under the collective ownership system. When the plant needed to recruit new workers in 1979, there was no quota for recruitment, so the plant was allowed to hire 300 workers under the collective ownership system. These workers then worked alongside the other workers and received the same pay and benefits. Now the plant has been asked to set up for these workers a separate factory, which will be responsible for its own

---

5/ Statistics from the plant's material supply section show that because of price increases, an extra 400,000 yuan was spent last year in purchasing coke, pig iron, rolled steel, nonferrous metal, timber and ancillary machinery and electrical products.

profits and losses. The plant is planning to assign 100 of these workers to a new can production line (see para. 6.12) and sign labor contracts with the remaining 200.

5.04 The contract workers were recruited in 1977. At that time, the plant was under the jurisdiction of the Changwei Prefectural Machine Building Bureau, which recruited the workers from the countryside under contracts renewable every three months. The recruitment of contract workers was included in the state plans. However, the plant may not recruit any additional contract workers.

5.05 Peasant workers were first recruited in 1975. With the objective of helping rural areas to train technical workers, the plant has since then recruited a total of 360 peasant workers (100 in 1975, 200 in 1976 and 60 in 1978). Contracts were signed for a five-year period, at the end of which the peasant workers would return to the countryside and not be replaced. The plant still has 47 peasant workers, who were to have been dismissed in August 1983 when their term ended. The plant will not recruit any more of these workers. The recruitment of peasant workers was not included in the state plans.

5.06 The plant also has an affiliated factory run by its workers' dependents, totalling 95 in all. The factory is registered with the country's Industrial Commercial Administration Bureau, holds its own business license, and is required to pay taxes. While it contracts with the plant to provide services and products, it also has the right to solicit work from other units.

Labor Issues

5.07 The present system for recruiting and dismissing staff gives rise to several problems. Firstly, in recruiting new workers, the plant is allocated a quota approved by the Municipal Labor Bureau. Recruitment is actually carried out by the county's Labor Bureau, which tests candidates, arranges for their medical examinations, and decides which ones to recruit and where to place them. The plant is not allowed to choose better qualified workers. Moreover, although the plant's production tasks require a male-female ratio of 70:30 among its workers, half of the workers allocated by the county are female (it is difficult for the plant to find jobs for so many women).

5.08 Secondly, the plant has a weak technical staff and too few college graduates. When it applied for college graduates for the first time last year, it had to go through the Municipal Machine-Building Bureau and Personnel Bureau up to the Provincial Machine-Building Bureau to obtain approval for an allocation of 12 graduates. Actually, the county kept 5 of these graduates and the plant got only 7, including one secondary vocational school graduate. In future, the plant plans to request more college graduates. In the meantime, to provide better training for its staff, the plant has established an educational committee and built a new training building. It has arranged for some staff to receive full-time training and has run three courses (each lasting a term) at the workers' spare-time college. However, to encourage staff to study and undertake training, the plant needs support from the relevant departments, in terms of recognition for the academic qualification of those who complete training and awarding appropriate titles and positions to those who acquire the qualifications of technical staff. So far 92 staff have graduated after completing three years of study and most have been (or will be) assigned to technical tasks.

5.09 Thirdly, the plant has limited power to deal with staff who have made serious mistakes. If it wants to release them permanently, it must obtain approval from the Municipal Machine-Building Bureau. It has the power to suspend them and put them on probation for a year, but is required to pay them 25 yuan each month for living expenses during that year and to reinstate them afterwards at their original wage level.

Wage System

5.10 The wage system implemented in the plant is the eight-grade wage system generally enforced in factories in China. The wages by grade level are shown below.

	State Ownership System	Collective Ownership System
Grade 1	30 yuan	30.8 yuan
Grade 2	35 yuan	36.1 yuan
Grade 3	41 yuan	42.3 yuan
Grade 4	48 yuan	49.4 yuan
Grade 5	56 yuan	57.8 yuan
Grade 6	66 yuan	67.6 yuan
Grade 7	77 yuan	79.2 yuan
Grade 8	90 yuan	92.5 yuan

As of January 1983, workers under the state ownership system had an average grade of 3.08 and an average monthly wage of 42.49 yuan. Workers under the collective ownership system were mostly in the first grade. The daily wage rate for contract workers is 1.48 yuan for men and 1.25 yuan for women. Peasant workers get 39 yuan per month in their first year, 41 yuan in their second, 43 in their third, and 45 yuan in their fourth and the fifth years. At the end of their contract they receive three months' pay. The plant pays two yuan per day for each worker in the affiliated factory, which actually pays 1.2 yuan per day to individual workers. Under the present wage system, workers of different categories generally start with more or less the same wages; there is little difference between grades and the gap between the highest and the lowest grades is acceptable.

5.11 There are three main issues concerning the present wage system. Firstly, the plant currently follows a time-rate wage system with a modified piece-rate bonus system for some workers. It achieved good results with a full-fledged piece-rate wage system before the Cultural Revolution, but its supervisary bureau does not agree to implementing a piece-rate wage system now. The plant's managers however, believe that restoration of this system would help to increase labor efficiency and that output value would double without additional equipment.

5.12 Secondly, the plant has also considered instituting a floating wage system, under which 20% of total basic wages would be for floating wages. However, this system would conflict with labor insurance regulations under which staff who are on sick leave for less than six months and who have completed eight years of service or more are to receive 100% of their wages. Under the suggested floating wage system, they would get only 80% of their basic wages. Similarly, workers who have fulfilled production quotas based on working hours would receive only 80% of the basic wage under the floating wage system. It would be difficult to implement a floating wage system for staff in the functional offices, which do not have fixed quotas. Moreover, setting aside 20% of basic wages for floating wages would create hardship for some staff, since wages are generally low. Thus, the introduction of a floating wage system is still under study. The plant would like to experiment with a contract system for service work.

5.13 Thirdly, the plant has no power to demote or promote staff, even though such actions, if they involve less than 1% of the wage bill, should be at the discretion of the director of the plant according to the regulations governing factory directors. The State Council decides whether wage adjustments should be made and issues directives accordingly, while the actual amount allocated for adjustments is determined by the supervisory bureau.

Economic Responsibility System

5.14 In order to provide a sound basis for evaluating performance, the plant introduced on July 1, 1982, an economic responsibility system described as the "five quotas", "three guarantees" and "three evaluation criteria" in both the workshops and the offices.

5.15 The "five quotas" are for the number of people, the number of machines, output, quality standards and profits in the case of workshops, and the number of people, posts, quality of work, amount of work and expenses in the case of offices.

5.16 The "three guarantees" refer to the three major indicators of output (including that of ancillary equipment), quality and profit which the plant has undertaken to fulfill as part of its economic responsibility to the state. These indicators are subdivided into smaller quotas for implementation by workshops, offices, work shifts or groups, and individuals. The workshops must meet the annual profit, output and quality targets set by the plant's management. Depending on the nature of their work, the offices must usually meet targets for the amount of work, profit and overhead expenses.

5.17 The "three evaluation criteria" refer to the three aspects of performance examined by the plant. The first criterion is the "three guarantees" against which the performance of workshops and offices is evaluated every month. The second criterion consists of ten standards of work expressed in percentage terms, including attendance, condition of equipment, safety and tidiness, cost of managing production processes, etc. The third criterion is the working relationship between the various units. It aims at improving the coordination between consecutive production processes, between different workshops, and between the workshops and offices, and at ensuring that individual staff will work to fulfill the quotas of their units, which will in turn help meet that of the plant.

5.18 Besides checking the indicators of output, quality and consumption, the workshop also evaluates the performance of work shifts and groups against a number of minor targets, such as attendance, recordkeeping, equipment maintenance, safety and spare-time study. Each of these targets has specific contents, requirements and method of evaluation.

5.19 In 1982 the plant started initial work to establish labor requirements for its various units. The workshops adjusted their production capacity based on their production tasks, and accordingly set norms for the numbers of people and machines required, output and consumption. As a result, the workshops dismissed 20 temporary workers and freed 33 technical staff for a workshop to develop new products. Despite staff reductions another 23 pieces of equipment were put into operation. The offices also made corresponding staff adjustments, and 20 workers returned to first-line production tasks.

5.20 Last year the plant also revised the norms for the number of hours' work required to produce its major products.[6/] The revised norms are advanced by the industry's general standards in China. In future, the plant plans to revise these norms once or twice a year.

Bonus Systems

5.21 As mentioned in para. 4.10, the plant implements two bonus systems, one on the basis of piece rates for staff in the production workshops, the other on the basis of time rates for staff in the supporting departments and offices. In 1982, there were 422 people under the latter system and 1,147 under the former. The average bonus was 135.20 yuan.

5.22 The piece-rate bonus system was introduced in 1981. Under this system, production quotas are given on the basis of working hours, which average 204 hours per person per month, and 0.22 yuan is paid for each hour's work above the quota. In 1982 the highest bonus received under this system was 550 yuan. The plant evaluates the performance of its workshops, which in turn evaluate the performance of the work shifts or groups.

5.23 Distribution coefficients for bonuses are set according to the economic contribution, importance of the job, technical complexity, labor intensity, and magnitude of the economic responsibility of the unit or individual. The plant's units and cadres are divided into nine grades, each with a different coefficient. For instance, the distribution coefficients for the director and deputy directors are 1.4 and 1.3, respectively. The coefficient for first-line production workshops (such as hot processing) is 1.2; for second-line production workshops (such as cold processing), 1.1; and for

---

6/ The norm for the 160T press was reduced by 2.5%; for the 300T press, by 3.23%; for the 400T press, by 1.32%; for the 630T press, by 1.6%; for the 1000T press, by 0.7%; and for the 1600T press, by 0.9%.

third-line production workshops, 0.9. Offices of the first category (i.e. those directly related to production) have a coefficient of 0.9 and those of the second category a coefficient of 0.8. The heads and deputies of the workshops and offices have coefficients higher than those for their units by 0.2 and 0.1, respectively. A coefficient of one is equivalent to a monthly bonus of 10 yuan. The lowest coefficient gives a bonus of 7 yuan and the highest, 14 yuan. If one of the three targets for output, quality and profit is not reached, the monthly bonus for the individual, work shift/group, office and workshop is reduced. The plant's director and deputy directors had their bonuses reduced last year.

5.24 Implementation of this system has improved production and management. Last year, only about 40-50 people did not receive bonuses, some because they took more than five days sick leave or failed to complete production tasks.

5.25 In addition, an amount equivalent to 1% of total wages is drawn from the enterprise fund at the end of each year for awards to workers. Last year, more than 270 people, or 15 percent of the total staff received such awards. Four cited as "pacesetters" received 150 yuan each, and six cited as "production experts" received 70 yuan each. The rest were cited as outstanding workers, with some receiving 7 yuan each, and some being awarded certificates and prizes.

Other Worker Benefits

5.26 The plant has done much to improve collective welfare and labor insurance for its workers (including staff). In the last few years, the plant has completed an average of about 2,000 square meters per year of new workers' housing. All workers now have housing. Those who came to the plant in 1961 have three-room apartments with a total floor space of 50 square meters (plus a kitchen); newlyweds have a living space of 14 square meters (plus a kitchen); college graduates recently allocated to the plant share one room between two; and singles share one room between four. Average per capita living space is 6.5 square meters. The rent is quite low, about 6 fen per square meter per month.

5.27 The collective welfare facilities of the plant include a canteen, a nursery, a hospital, a public bath house, a cold storage room and a cultural club. The plant gives its staff subsidies for hair-cuts, baths and transport each month, and for heating costs every winter. Last year, 20,000 yuan of subsidies were distributed to workers in financial difficulties.

5.28 State regulations guarantee workers free medical care, while half of their dependents' medical fees are subsidized. Workers on sick leave receive full pay for the first six months, after which they receive 60% of their basic wages paid out of the labor insurance fund. In case of death, the labor insurance regulations require the plant to give a lump sum equivalent to 6, 9 or 12 months of basic wages to the directly related dependents. However, this amount is so small that the family of the deceased often finds itself in financial difficulty. In such cases the plant prefers to follow the regulations for government agencies, which require that the aged (the parents) be supported until they die and the young (the children) until they reach adulthood.

6. TECHNICAL TRANSFORMATION AND THE DEVELOPMENT OF NEW PRODUCTS

Technical Transformation

6.01 The Qingdao Forging Machinery Plant possesses 507 sets of machines and equipment,[7/] a gross value of 12.77 million yuan. The plant attaches great importance to the management and maintenance of this equipment. A team of managers and workers works full time to keep the equipment in good condition, to improve its performance, reduce downtime and extend its useful life, so that it will run well for a long time.

6.02 However, much of the plant's equipment was technically out of date and urgently needed to be remodeled and updated. In recent years, the plant has made great progress in this regard, remodeling and updating 38 pieces of equipment each in 1980 and 1982, and 35 pieces in 1981. The Shandong Provincial Machine-Building Bureau placed the plant ahead of 52 machine-building enterprises in the province for technical transformation. To date, 90% of the plant's small equipment has been remodeled, but partly due to shortage of funds, technical transformation of large equipment has been postponed.

6.03 Much of the large equipment now in use (such as the double housing planers and overhead cranes) was made by the plant itself and has been in use for 10-20 years. The key to technological reform now lies with the double housing planers, which are the major equipment item in manufacturing the frame and body of presses. Because some parts of the planer are higher than its crossbeam, its efficiency is very low. Using these planers, over 40,000 hours are spent each year in manufacturing the frame and body of presses (this is about one-seventh of the total number of working hours in the plant). Fitting milling cutters onto the planers would increase efficiency by 20-30%. Moreover, much energy would be saved and generating capacity could be reduced from 120 kw to 30 kw. Remodeling one planer would cost an estimated 60,000 to 70,000 yuan, of which about 50,000 yuan would be for the milling cutter (buying a double housing milling machine would cost about 200,000 yuan). By remodeling the planer, the plant would be able to increase its income by 20,000 to 30,000 yuan each year through savings in terms of improved efficiency and energy conservation, and the total cost of converting the planer could be recovered within three years. Shortage of funds for technical transformation has so far prevented this improvement from being made.

7/ This includes 49 sets of major equipment, 211 sets of metal cutting equipment, 18 sets of forging equipment, 55 sets of lifting and transport equipment, 11 sets of die-casting equipment, 14 sets of power equipment, 26 sets of electrical equipment and 11 furnaces and kilns.

6.04 Other obstacles to technical transformation are the lack of technical information, especially about foreign technology, and shortages of technical staff. The total staff assigned to technological development is less than 30, or about 2% of the plant's total staff.

6.05 The plant's managers believe that if they can successfully solve the problems of funding, information and technical training of staff, they will be able to carry out the technical transformation of existing equipment effectively, develop new products, increase production capacity and reduce the consumption of raw materials. They believe that through such intensive growth, the plant will be able to quadruple its output value by 1987 with no increase in personnel and equipment.

Development of New Products

6.06 Developing new products is also an urgent task. Although there is still a domestic market for the plant's friction presses, they should be replaced - in the interests of industrial development and in view of the more advanced technology available internationally - by newer, more efficient models. As with technical transformation, the plant's efforts in this area have been hampered by shortages of funds and technical personnel.

6.07 The plant has produced twin-disc friction presses for more than two decades. In the past, the plant had no incentive to improve or upgrade its products: the presses became outdated and were inefficient in their use of energy and materials. After the readjustment program started in 1979, the plant conducted market surveys and learned that sales of its products had stagnated not because of lack of demand but because its products were obsolete and their designs no longer met users' needs.

6.08 In the last few years, the plant has programmed its research and new product development to suit the demand for technical transformation in light industry. It organized a technical team to design and manufacture a 160T twin-disc friction press for the cutlery industry. This new press, which is used for cold pressing and precision forging in tableware production, is efficient, safe and labor-saving. For the bicycle industry, the plant developed a 630 T horizontal, multi-position, cold extrusion press used in making such parts as the mudguard and brake shoes. This press can reduce raw materials requirements by 20% and improve efficiency by 50%; it can also increase the precision of the manufactured parts, reduce wear on cutters, and help improve working conditions in the bicycle industry. The plant has also designed and manufactured for a thermos factory a 63 T punch, which is compact, efficient and has a long stroke. As mentioned, the plant now provides complete production lines rather than just single machines.

6.09 The plant has used various means to solicit the views of customers on the adaptability, reliability and durability of its products. It has grouped the comments it received into 5 major categories and identified 49 key problems; it has organized six special teams to tackle individual problems. So far, it has remodeled light friction presses such as the 160T, 300T and 400T models, which are now lighter, quieter, better-designed and easier to operate. The plant is also using its technical staff to improve the quality and technical performance of its heavy presses.

6.10 The plant is also assessing its development potential over the long term. It has placed major emphasis on the design of a new drive mechanism to replace that used in the twin-disc friction press, since this is outdated and inefficient, causes high friction loss and high energy consumption, and has a low stroke frequency. The plant's efforts over the last few years have led to some initial success in designing a 10T two-way spiral press, a 100T high-energy press and 160T high-efficiency and energy-saving press. These new products mark a major breakthrough in the mode of transmission, eliminating two friction discs and using an electric motor to move the drive wheel. They are also compact, lightweight, highly efficient, versatile, and energy-saving. These technical innovations should ensure continuity of production once demand for the twin disc friction press is exhausted.

6.11 However, the plant has also encountered difficulties in developing new products, mainly a shortage of funds. Except for projects directly assigned by the relevant ministries or commissions in the central government (for which the plant would be allocated sufficient funds and assured of a certain proportion of profits), the plant does not have adequate financing to develop new products either to expand the range of its production or to conduct technical research to prepare for future growth. Funds for research and trial production allocated by higher authorities and payments made by customers fall short of actual expenses.[8/] Even if the plant could use an amount equivalent to 3% of sales revenue (the amount allowed for the machine-building industry) for the trial production of new products, this would not cover total expenses incurred. Moreover, it costs more to produce better quality new products than existing models, which together with price increases for raw materials has resulted in higher production costs. However, as mentioned, the price of the improved product cannot increase and may even be reduced. Thus under current conditions, the more new products a plant develops, the higher the losses it incurs. This outcome needs to be reversed if this work is to continue.

6.12 The plant also has difficulty in obtaining loans for developing new products. For example in early 1982, it learned from the Ministry of Light Industry that the export of beer and other beverages has been adversely affected by the backward technology used to make their containers, which are three-piece welded tin cans used since the 1950s. Beverage containers popular in the international market are the high-frequency resistance welded cans, which are air-tight, can be stored for a long time, are produced at low cost and are easy to open. After consulting the relevant departments, the plant decided to try and develop a production line for this kind of can. The complete line would require 13 sets of equipment. Design work is now well under way and the plant plans to complete the first production line soon. It will then make test-runs to prepare for the production of equipment for similar production lines in the future; at the same time, it will be producing new beer cans. In

---

8/ For instance, the plant spent 94,100 yuan in developing the 100T high-energy press and the 10T two-way forging press, but was only allocated 30,000 yuan by higher authorities, thus incurring a loss of 64,100 yuan.

this way, the plant will be able not only to improve the beverage canning industry in China, but also to increase its own economic returns. The plant has estimated that two years from now, it will be able to more than double its output value and almost triple its profits. This project was approved by the packaging committee under the Ministry of Machine Building, which agreed to allocate the plant a loan of 1.2 million yuan from its 1982 loan quotas. However, an objection from the provincial People's Bank has prevented the plant from receiving this loan. The plant has already spent more than 100,000 yuan in developing and designing the new production line. It plans to continue discussing this matter with the provincial People's Bank. However, this situation reveals that under the new system for capital construction investment, in which grants are replaced by loans, disagreements between the supervisory bureau/ministry and the bank can hinder the granting of loans and hence prevent the start of some urgently needed projects.

6.13 Thus, through its own efforts, the plant has in recent years made some progress in developing new products, but it faces many difficulties. To cover the cost of developing new products, the products must be reasonably priced and the enterprise given a reasonable share of profits.

Statistical Appendix A

Chongqing Clock & Watch Company

ENTERPRISE MANAGEMENT STUDY QUESTIONNAIRE

Quantitative Data

Item	Units	1975	1976	1977	1978	1979	1980	1981	1982
I. Production									
1. Gross value of industrial output (at 1970 prices)	10,000 yuan	619.40	644.99	1314.01	2358.91	3088.64	5327.71	8522.81	8854.28
2. Gross value of industrial output (at current prices)	10,000 yuan	486.56	1572.76	1492.41	1973.02	2563.13	4470.88	7364.23	6397.36
3. Net value of industrial output (at current prices)	10,000 yuan	-	-	500.20	1120.64	1559.11	2763.70	4213.47	4000.00
4. Physical output of main industrial commodities produced									
a. Watch	10,000 units	0.3989	0.8774	7.0000	18.1168	28.0000	50.1210	80.0000	88.3923
b. Alarm clock	" "	48.1350	38.1500	55.6770	65.4406	70.0416	100.0158	121.0183	54.15205
5. Value of output of main industrial commodities produced									
a. Watch (in 1970 constant prices)	10,000 yuan	-	68.44	546.00	1413.11	2184.00	3781.35	5970.76	6892.56
b. Alarm clock (in 1970 constant prices)	" "	-	529.48	419.60	612.45	719.85	770.44	1091.61	585.34

Item	Units	1975	1976	1977	1978	1979	1980	1981	1982
II. Labor Force									
6. Total wage bill (regular staff)*	yuan	810,073	886,600	978,182	1,341,821	1,836,645	2,949,997	3,174,246	3,335,220
Of which: Time-rate wages	"	-	-	-	1,073,070	1,237,412	1,802,831	1,827,340	2,304,472
Piece-rate wages	"	-	-	-	-	-	-	40,010	-
Overtime wages	"	-	-	-	48,610	47,494	211,131	347,882	137,334
Supplementary wages	"	-	-	-	19,278	23,284	29,138	18,268	8,507
Subsidies	"	-	-	-	72,202	103,008	312,859	482,569	332,198
Bonuses charged to production costs	"	-	-	-	128,661	297,853	408,361	383,586	496,033
7. Labor insurance expenditures	yuan	-	-	-	40,154	48,683	103,698	125,458	157,344
8. Collective welfare expenditure for workers and staff	yuan	-	-	-	162,379	255,577	325,553	490,838	633,132
9. Total number of workers and staff (average during the year)	person	1,515	1,746	1,948	2,501	2,654	3,787	3,978	4,287
a. Temporary workers (average during the year)	person	23	20	27	246	54	486	560	512
b. Regular workers (average during the year)**	person	1,492	1,726	1,921	2,255	2,600	3,301	3,418	3,775

* Does not include wages for temporary workers.
** Figures provided here are for all regular staff.

Item	Units /a	1975	1976	1977	1978	1979	1980	1981	1982
c. Apprentices (average during year)	person	33	332	420	572	271	190	242	237
d. Engineers and technicians (average during year)	person	76	71	68	86	78	202	160	172
e. Managerial personnel (average during year)	person	70	95	96	214	274	288	586	561
f. Service personnel (average during year)	person	84	96	108	150	179	260	299	267
g. Other staff (average during year)	person	14	52	55	73	138	190	158	147
10. Average wages per employee *	yuan	543	514	509	595	706	894	929	884
a. Temporary workers	yuan	-	-	-	-	-	-	-	-
b. Regular workers **	"	543	514	509	595	706	894	929	884
c. Apprentices	"	228	204	228	276	360	420	468	454
d. Engineers and technicians	"	720	720	720	840	906	960	1,008	1,004
e. Managerial personnel	"	564	540	840	680	725	795	834	829
f. Service personnel	"	1,540	1,540	1,504	624	720	750	828	820
g. Other staff	"	360	324	324	420	1,540	600	636	630

* For regular staff only.
** Figures provided here are for all regular staff.

Item	Units	1975	1976	1977	1978	1979	1980	1981	1982
III. Fixed Assets									
11. Original value of fixed assets at year-end	10,000 yuan	1377.41	1679.28	2160.31	2243.21	2723.61	3189.22	3981.33	6370.27
Of which: Machinery & equipment	" "	1268.98	1466.90	1769.33	1836.69	2170.82	2392.89	2824.03	4256.78
Buildings	" "	108.43	212.38	390.98	406.152	1551.73	797.27	1156.24	2112.43
Other	" "	-	-	-	-	1.06	1.06	1.06	1.06
12. Net book value of fixed assets at year-end +	10,000 yuan	1214.89	1460.43	1880.32	1868.91	2116.23	2477.09	3156.31	5444.68
13. Utilization rates for main types of machinery and equipment (in percent)									
a. Automatic cars (90-95%) *	set**	65	78	90	110	120	127	154	249
b. Equipment for jaws (60%) and cases	set	161	180	196	215	251	285	310	346
c. Equipment for movement(60%) parts	set	40	45	45	55	65	70	96	155
d. Equipment for general (80%) assembly	set	36	45	60	75	85	100	120	176
e. Equipment for support (60%) services	set	120	160	206	235	270	310	330	381

+ i.e., net fixed asset value.
* Percentages designate the proportion of machinery and equipment in use
** Number of sets of each type of machines/equipment.

Item	Units	1975	1976	1977	1978	1979	1980	1981	1982
IV. Circulating Assets									
14. Total value of quota circulating assets at year-end	10,000 yuan	490.81	635.74	775.84	885.64	1297.58	1573.34	2116.92	2769.10
Of which: inputs +	" "	354.84	435.85	522.86	650.74	796.90	1001.77	1152.25	1468.30
goods in process +	" "	110.63	178.52	191.64	175.55	270.05	413.01	579.50	876.40
outputs +	" "	25.34	21.37	61.34	58.33	145.89	158.56	385.17	424.40
15. Total value of non-quota circulating assets at year-end	10,000 yuan	60.05	88.58	43.22	59.55	63.08	193.94	176.65	347.65
Of which: Cash	" "	0.02	0.00	0.04	0.04	0.06	0.11	0.14	0.06
Bank deposits	" "	18.46	8.21	19.40	37.74	30.06	31.36	13.36	9.42
Receivables	" "	41.57	80.37	23.78	21.77	32.96	162.47	163.15	338.17
Other	" "	-	-	-	-	-	-	-	-

+ Equivalent to reserve fund, production fund and final products in Chinese terms.

Item	Units	1975	1976	1977	1978	1979	1980	1981	1982
V. Investment									
16. Total capital construction investment (current prices)	10,000 yuan	319.45	302.12	481.02	53.15	7.06	100.08	-	-
a. Breakdown by type of investment									
- Civil construction	" "	22.26	103.95	178.60	15.54	-	33.25	-	-
- Machinery, equip., implements	" "	297.19	198.17	302.42	37.61	7.06	66.83	-	-
- Other	" "	-	-	-	-	-	-	-	-
b. Breakdown by source of financing		319.45	302.12	481.02	53.15	7.06	100.08	-	-
- State budget appropriations	" "								
- Capital construction loans	" "								
- Enterprise's own funds	" "								
- Grants or loans from local government	" "								
- Other	" "								
17. Investment for renewal and modernization of fixed assets	10,000 yuan	-	-	-	38.40	249.01	395.83	854.80	2499.63
a. Breakdown by type of investment									
- Civil construction	" "	-	-	-	18.00	-	190.03	199.19	961.92
- Machinery, equip., implements	" "	-	-	-	20.40	249.01	205.80	655.61	1537.71
- Other	" "	-	-	-	-	-	-	-	-

Item	Units	1975	1976	1977	1978	1979	1980	1981	1982
b. Breakdown by source of financing +	10,000 yuan	____	____	____	38.40	249.01	395.83	854.80	2499.63
- State budget appropriations ++	" "	____	____	____	27.18	1.40	-	195.97	328.65
- Depreciation funds	" "	____	____	____	-	208.19	61.50	25.38	141.70
- Enterprise retained profits	" "	____	____	____	-	-	68.31	-	961.37
- Short- and medium-term loans for equipment purchase									
- from People's Bank of China	" "	____	____	____	-	-	41.16	429.80	589.78
- from People's Construction Bank of China *	" "	____	____	____	11.22	-	97.49	-	-
- from Bank of China	" "	____	____	____	-	-	-	-	283.13
- from other banks	" "	____	____	____	-	-	-	-	-
- Other sources of financing **	" "	____	____	____	-	39.42	127.37	203.65	195.00

\+ In all cases the value of completed investments in a year [which began to be counted as fixed assets in that year] is taken to be the amount of investment for that year, although the funds were not actually received [and invested] in that year.

++ Include specialization subsidies from higher levels, new product trial production funds, etc.

* Used to cover cost of domestically produced complement parts for imported equipment.

** Include funds for major repairs and loans from local finances (municipal government loans).

Item	Units	1975	1976	1977	1978	1979	1980	1981	1982
VI. Financial Indicators									
18. Total revenues from sales of products (at current prices)	10,000 yuan	557.11	560.54	1043.10	2047.68	2808.74	4257.02	6664.10	5641.37
19. Total costs of products *	10,000 yuan	421.35	424.03	670.34	1090.33	1473.58	1987.60	3492.00	2825.15
Of which: Production costs	" "	421.35	424.03	670.34	1090.33	1473.58	1987.60	3416.78	2787.48
Marketing costs	" "								
Taxes +	" "	129.12	120.12	266.70	658.32	897.57	1228.90	1622.21	1646.55
20. Net profits from sales of commodities (18 minus 19)	10,000 yuan	6.64	16.40	106.07	299.03	437.58	1040.51	1549.90	1169.67
21. Net profits from economic activities other than commodity sales**	10,000 yuan	-	-	-	-	0.48	52.65	80.11	39.05
22. Net expenditures on non-profit activities++	10,000 yuan	0.50	15.97	3.152	8.93	10.98	61.81	-65.91	55.24
23. Administrative profits (20 plus 21 minus 22)	10,000 yuan	6.14	0.43	102.54	290.10	427.08	1031.35	1695.91	1153.48
24. Distribution of admin. profits	10,000 yuan	6.14	0.43	102.54	290.10	427.08	1031.35	1695.91	1153.48
a. Repayment of bank loans for fixed investment	" "	-	-	13.57	29.86	0.00	27.40	293.00	514.57
b. Remitted to higher levels	" "	5.94	0.04	89.17	253.24	374.16	-	-	-
c. Tax payments (other than those in no. 19)+++	" "	-	-	-	-	-	490.61	659.27	391.90

* Includes production and marketing costs.
\+ i.e., the industrial commercial tax.
** Includes other sales of material and profit not entered in the previous year.
++ i.e., non-operational expenses (in 1981, in a general financial check up, the value of inventory of goods in process was Y 1,238,000).
+++ i.e., income tax.

Item	Units	1975	1976	1977	1978	1979	1980	1981	1982
d. Fee for state-owned fixed assets (if any)	10,000 yuan	-	-	-	-	-	66.35	80.93	0.00*
e. Fee for state-owned circulating assets (if any)	" "	-	-	-	-	-	-	-	12.33
f. Retained by enterprise	" "	-	-	-	6.46	56.08	431.98	662.71	234.68
g. Other	" "	-	-	-	-	-	15.00	-	-
25. Uses of enterprise retained profits +									
a. Total profits retained by enterprise during the year	10,000 yuan	-	-	-	6.46	56.08	431.98	662.71	234.68
- Used for production development expenditures	" "	-	-	-	3.88	33.65	359.19	397.63	140.81
- Used for worker's collective welfare expenditures	" "	-	-	-	1.93	16.82	129.59	198.81	70.40
- Used for worker's bonuses	" "	-	-	-	0.65	5.61	43.20	66.27	23.47
- Used for other purposes	" "	-	-	-	-	-	-	-	-
b. Net change in accumulated balance of retained profits held by the enterprise	" "	-	-	-	-	-	-	-	-
26. Depreciation funds generated during the year	10,000 yuan	25.42	56.04	61.13	95.09	112.94	115.21	124.23	142.48
Of which: retained by enterprise	" "	10.07	22.42	24.45	47.54	64.94	80.65	86.96	99.74

* Requested for exemption.

\+ In five years, total expenses for production development was Y 8,351,600; for collective welfare for staff and workers, Y 4,175,500, of which Y 1,945,200 was for civil works and Y 2,230,300 for welfare (small items). The proportion of bonuses for staff and workers in these five years was 10% [of retained profits], or Y 1,392,000 which, however, was not paid out as bonus but used for collective welfare for staff and workers.

Item	Units	1975	1976	1977	1978	1979	1980	1981	1982
VII. Planning									
27. Annual gross output value									
a. Planned value promulgated	10,000 yuan	484.00	922.00	1020.00	1530.00	2624.00	3300.00	6000.00	1,0150.00
b. Revised value in annual plan	" "	-	-	930.00	1850.00	-	-	-	8000.00
c. Value achieved	" "	619.40	644.99	1314.01	2358.91	3088.64	5327.17	8522.81	8854.28
28. Annual total profits									
a. Planned value promulgated	10,000 yuan	5.00	50.00	75.00	250.00	294.00	822.00	1350.00	1800.00
b. Revised value in annual plan	" "	5.00	50.00	75.00	250.00	294.00	822.00	1350.00	1150.00
c. Value achieved	" "	6.14	0.43	102.54	290.10	427.08	1031.35	1695.91	1153.48
29. Profits handed over to higher level									
a. Planned value promulgated	10,000 yuan	5.00	50.00	75.00	250.00	264.00	539.00	650.00	-
b. Revised value in annual plan	" "	5.00	50.00	75.00	250.00	264.00	539.00	730.00	-
c. Value achieved	" "	-5.94	0.04	89.17	253.24	374.16	556.96	740.20	404.23

Item	Units	1975	1976	1977	1978	1979	1980	1981	1982
VIII. Input Consumption									
30. Ratios of material input consumption to output produced of major commodities	kg/10,000 units								
a. copper per 10,000 alarm clocks	" "	1790	1780	1760	1758	1734	1670	1684	1657
b. steel per 10,000 alarm clocks	" "	4340	4300	3850	3871	3791	3779	3737	3709
c. copper per 10,000 watches	" "	-	-	-	1469	1442	999	837	861
d. steel per 10,000 watches	" "	-	-	-	1667	1551	1237	1077	1092
31. Energy consumption									
Total consumption of electricity during year	kWh	145.30	125.54	242.32	273.14	327.40	477.29	551.41	589.57
Of which: Power consumed in industrial production	kWh	138.50	119.29	230.00	259.48	314.59	409.60	475.03	528.31
Total consumption of coal during year *	ton	1240.00	703.00	28.70	154.30	41.40	657.50	704.00	579.20
Total consumption of fuel oil during year	ton	___	___	___	___	___	___	___	___

* Including a small amount for residential use.

Item	Units /a	1975	1976	1977	1978	1979	1980	1981	1982
IX. Inventories									
32. Year-end inventories of major outputs									
a. Watch	unit	1643.00	574.00	10700.00	6.065	1705.00	10948.00	14737.00	22371.00
b. Alarm clock	unit	13598.00	6023.00	15009.00	21152.00	38523.00	89523.00	185337.00	362105.00
33. Year-end inventories of major inputs									
a. Coal	ton	387	115	3	9	126	6	-	-
b. Fuel (gasoline for transportation)	"	9	5	4	23	18	21	9	27
c. Steel	"	421	495	333	523	541	878	626	932
d. Others (copper)	"	165	218	220	195	275	206	258	442

Statistical Appendix B

Qingdao Forging Machinery Plant

Item	Units	1965	1973	1975	1976	1977	1978	1979	1980	1981	1982
I. Production											
1. Gross value of industrial output (at 1970 prices)	Y 10,000	329.52	1,200.57	1,708.74	2,280.03	2,573.21	1,890.32	2,109.31	2,088.37	1,655.49	1,735.66
2. Gross value of industrial output (at current prices)	Y 10,000	372.03	1,161.57	1,679.62	2,175.08	2,336.67	1,825.43	1,899.26	1,914.67	1,601.99	1,618.40
3. Net value of industrial output (at current prices)	Y 10,000	-	-	-	-	484.17	474.48	528.00	523.40	442.83	435.34
4. Physical output of main industrial commodities produced	set										
a. J53-160B press	"	40	36	36	40	30	37	35	30	65	58
b. J53-300 press	"	30	124	100	110	80	91	100	110	100	135
c. J53-400 press	"	-	15	27	45	60	63	49	25	33	30
d. J53-630 press	"	-	3	10	10	5	12	15	19	1	15
5. Value of output of main industrial commodities produced (at 1970 prices)											
a. J53-160B press	Y 10,000	64.00	57.60	57.60	64.00	38.00	59.20	56.00	48.00	104.00	72.80
b. J53-300 press	"	90.00	372.00	300.00	330.00	240.00	273.00	318.00	330.00	300.00	405.00
c. J53-400 press	"	-	120.00	216.00	360.00	480.00	504.00	392.00	200.00	264.00	240.00
d. J53-630 press	"	-	75.00	250.00	250.00	125.00	300.00	375.00	475.00	25.00	375.00

Item	Units	1965	1973	1975	1976	1977	1978	1979	1980	1981	1982
II. Labor Force											
6. Total wage bill	Y 10,000	17.75	49.75	54.55	54.51	60.22	78.78	99.91	112.34	130.70	115.88
Of which: Time-rate wages Piece-rate wages	") ")	-	43.09	46.66	47.60	48.65	69.83	71.29	69.43	49.62 31.13	23.38 53.57
Overtime wages	"	-	2.70	4.40	3.70	7.37	4.86	2.94	3.19	3.39	2.63
Supplementary wages	"	-	1.65	1.63	1.51	1.47	0.76	1.42	1.27	0.96	0.97
Subsidies	"	-	2.31	1.86	1.70	2.73	3.33	7.58	16.47	16.46	17.74
Bonuses charged to production costs	"	-	-	-	-	-	-	16.68	21.97	29.14	17.59
7. Labor insurance expenditures	Y 10,000	-	0.58	2.62	2.75	8.80	2.99	3.27	3.90	6.27	7.19
8. Collective welfare expenditure for workers and staff	Y 10,000	-	5.86	0.22	6.30	8.70	8.60	9.36	10.73	14.93	10.27
9. Total number of workers and staff (average during the year)		310	985	1,008	1,030	1,089	1,467	1,502	1,709	1,616	1,561
a. Temporary workers (average during the year)	person	4	2	-	19	32	397	400	321	210	88
b. Regular workers (average during the year)	"	224	677	854	765	747	726	736	720	754	853
c. Apprentices (average during year)	"	2	171	11	39	60	51	26	266	231	194
d. Engineers and technicians (average during year)	"	24	29	27	42	47	63	66	83	87	87
e. Managerial personnel (average during year)	"	44	47	55	106	139	163	179	183	185	193
f. Service personnel (average during year)	"	11	54	57	55	56	59	68	94	102	106
g. Other staff (average during year)	"	1	5	4	4	8	8	27	42	47	40

Item	Units	1965	1973	1975	1976	1977	1978	1979	1980	1981	1982
II. Labor Force (Cont'd)											
10. Average wages per employee	Y	573	505	541	529	553	537	665	657	809	742
a. Temporary workers	"	462	257	-	452	479	519	591	711	840	641
b. Regular workers	"	544	540	540	530	556	600	711	803	856	774
c, Apprentices	"	369	306	282	274	277	240	452	506	572	464
d. Engineers and technicians	"	733	669	608	621	673	567	798	805	924	899
e. Managerial personnel	"	653	675	650	643	656	491	764	936	930	848
f. Service personnel	"	559	455	477	450	506	486	637	695	705	658
g. Other staff	"	552	227	390	358	348	386	443	465	599	589
III. Fixed Assets											
11. Original value of fixed assets at year-end	Y 10,000	233.71	991.97	1,268.16	1,383.75	1,477.84	1,608.04	1,752.36	1,925.34	2,062.67	2,089.00
Of which: Nonproductive fixed assets	"	8.63	28.51	44.44	52.12	84.09	84.65	91.36	81.09	123.66	126.02
Productive fixed assets	"	210.68	959.16	1,219.36	1,330.67	1,388.77	1,518.41	1,593.51	1,776.33	1,863.23	1,827.31
Of which: Machinery & equipment) Buildings)	"	210.68	959.16	1,219.36	1,330.67	1,388.77	1,365.66	1,593.51	1,776.33	1,863.23	1,688.43
Other	"	14.39	4.30	4.37	4.37	4.99	4.49	108.85	67.93	75.78	135.67
12. Net book value of fixed assets at year-end	Y 10,000	175.89	743.71	930.68	989.07	1,023.36	1,089.43	1,133.84	1,296.43	1,353.63	1,305.99
13. Utilization rates for main types of machinery and equipment (in percent)	%										
a. Metal cutting lathe	"	83.80	68.60	59.60	56.70	65.80	62.20	55.30	53.69	47.56	46.98
b. Forging equipment	"	-	-	-	29.00	-	35.76	27.40	20.50	16.40	20.30

Item	Units	1965	1973	1975	1976	1977	1978	1979	1980	1981	1982
IV. Circulating Assets											
14. Total value of quota circulating assets at year-end	Y 10,000	115.77	1,041.06	1,188.10	1,582.30	1,824.10	2,365.60	1,788.70	1,877.10	1,532.20	1,400.70
Of which: inputs (reserve fund)	"	104.21	732.70	737.40	851.40	1,057.90	1,365.10	1,084.50	1,013.70	716.50	698.30
goods in process (production fund)	"	8.86	230.87	368.40	583.00	478.80	851.20	579.20	663.10	727.80	612.00
outputs (final products)	"	2.70	77.49	82.30	147.90	287.40	149.30	125.00	200.30	87.90	90.40
15. Total value of non-quota circulating assets at year-end	Y 10,000	41.90	29.91	57.42	56.54	214.36	169.18	266.46	139.78	138.59	293.98
Of which: Cash	"	0.11	0.16	0.15	0.14	0.08	0.09	0.10	0.04	0.16	0.07
Bank deposits	"	12.37	4.39	30.80	6.22	11.27	3.80	5.47	8.18	4.49	29.02
Other	"	8.09	-	9.32	-	149.88	74.50	176.01	21.88	66.78	96.67
16. Receivables at year-end	Y 10,000	21.44	25.36	17.15	50.18	52.41	90.79	84.88	109.68	67.16	168.22
Payables at year-end	"	11.45	199.51	285.60	403.71	466.73	872.21	338.30	378.10	184.47	100.11

Item	Units	1965	1973	1975	1976	1977	1978	1979	1980	1981	1982
V. Investment											
17. Total capital construction investment (current prices)	Y 10,000	-	-	221.67	63.50	127.80	69.00	12.80	50.18	38.00	3.00
a. Breakdown by type of investment											
- Civil construction	"	-	-	5.24	41.50	88.80	69.40	12.80	43.18	38.00	3.00
- Machinery, equip., implements	"	-	-	216.43	22.00	39.00	-	-	7.00	-	-
- Other	"	-	-	-	-	-	-	-	-	-	-
b. Breakdown by source of financing											
- State budget appropriations	"	-	-	-	51.50	5.00	60.00	12.80	-	-	-
- Capital construction loans	"	-	-	-	-	-	-	-	-	-	-
- Enterprise's own funds	"	-	-	221.67	12.00	123.80	9.00	-	50.18	38.00	3.00
- Grants or loans from local Gov't	"	-	-	-	-	-	-	-	-	-	-
- Other	"	-	-	-	-	-	-	-	-	-	-
18. Investment for renewal and modernization of fixed assets	Y 10,000	-	-	66.50	52.20	111.54	116.40	44.08	68.62	115.54	62.33
a. Breakdown by type of investment											
- Civil construction	"	-	-	13.36	1.20	51.20	55.29	7.00	21.85	75.72	20.00
- Machinery, equip., implements	"	-	-	53.14	51.00	60.34	61.11	37.08	40.38	39.82	42.23
- Other	"	-	-	-	-	-	-	-	6.39	-	-
b. Breakdown by source of financing											
- State budget appropriations	"	-	-	13.60	5.00	29.70	6.00	-	-	-	5.00
- Depreciation funds	"	-	-	33.53	23.20	63.40	67.70	29.47	66.50	101.04	-
- Enterprise retained profits	"	-	-	-	-	-	-	-	-	14.50	-
- Grants or loans from local Gov't	"	-	-	-	-	-	38.00	-	2.00	-	35.00
- Short- and medium-term loans for equipment purchase											
- from People's Bank of China	"	-	-	-	-	-	-	-	-	-	-
- from People's Construction Bank of China	"	-	-	-	-	-	-	-	-	-	-
- from Bank of China	"	-	-	-	-	-	-	-	-	-	-
- from other banks	"	-	-	-	-	-	-	-	-	-	-
- Other sources of financing	"	-	-	19.37	24.00	18.44	4.70	14.61	-	-	27.23

Item	Units	1965	1973	1975	1976	1977	1978	1979	1980	1981	1982
VI. Financial Indicators											
19. Total revenues from sales of products (at current prices)	Y 10,000	352.88	1,021.09	1,317.67	1,238.68	1,852.40	1,884.38	2,047.69	1,965.36	1,536.25	1,674.38
20. Total costs of same	Y 10,000	268.38	818.98	1,109.08	1,031.45	1,566.30	1,643.00	1,776.08	1,696.44	1,352.07	1,511.05
Of which: Production costs	"	251.16	767.93	1,043.20	969.52	1,488.14	1,556.47	1,684.20	1,624.21	1,299.16	1,430.91
Marketing costs	"	-	-	-	-	-	-	-	-	-	-
Taxes	"	17.22	51.05	65.88	61.93	78.16	86.53	91.88	72.23	52.91	80.14
21. Net profits from sales of commodities (19 minus 20)	"	84.50	202.11	208.59	207.23	286.10	241.38	271.61	268.92	184.18	163.33
22. Net profits from economic activities other than commodity sales	"	2.41	14.10	24.34	12.08	12.75	13.67	33.79	2.58	55.40	4.54
23. Net expenditures on non-profit activities	Y 10,000	21.05	0.57	2.61	2.73	8.78	2.99	3.84	4.30	107.37	6.31
24. Administrative profits (21 plus 22 minus 23)	"	65.86	215.64	230.32	216.58	290.07	252.07	301.56	267.20	132.21	161.56

Item	Units	1965	1973	1975	1976	1977	1978	1979	1980	1981	1982
VI. Financial Indicators (Cont'd)											
25. Distribution of admin. profits	Y 10,000	65.86	215.64	230.32	216.58	290.07	252.07	301.56	267.20	132.21	161.56
a. Repayment of bank loans for fixed investment	"	7.48	22.85	10.00	10.00	-	75.00	-	-	-	-
b. Remitted to higher levels	"	57.03	192.79	220.32	206.58	290.07	237.07	271.43	256.05	96.81	138.37
c. Tax payments (other than those in no. 20)	"	-	-	-	-	-	-	-	-	-	-
d. Fee for state-owned fixed assets (if any)	"	-	-	-	-	-	-	-	-	-	-
e. Fee for state-owned circulatin assets (if any)	"	-	-	-	-	-	-	-	3.07	11.15	10.85
f. Retained by enterprise		1.27	-	-	-	-	-	30.13	8.08	24.25	12.40
g. Other	"	0.08	-	-	-	-	-	-	-	-	-
26. Uses of enterprise retained profits	Y 10,000										
a. Total profits retained by enterprise during the year	"	1.27	-	-	-	-	-	30.13	8.08	24.25	12.40
- Used for production development expenditures	"	-	-	-	-	-	-	-	-	14.50	7.44
- Used for worker's collective welfare expenditures	"	1.27	-	-	-	-	-	10.07	-	7.25	3.72
- Used for worker's bonuses	"	-	-	-	-	-	-	9.06	8.08	2.50	1.24
- Used for other purposes	"	-	-	-	-	-	-	11.00	-	-	-
b. Net change in accumulated balance of retained profits held by the enterprise	"	-	-	-	-	-	-	-	-	-	-
27. Depreciation funds generated during the year	Y 10,000	12.31	50.59	47.90	58.08	63.42	67.74	73.67	79.49	84.84	89.45
Of which: retained by enterprise	"	-	50.59	33.53	23.23	38.05	33.87	51.57	31.79	33.94	35.78

Item	Units	1965	1973	1975	1976	1977	1978	1979	1980	1981	1982
VII. Planning											
28. Annual gross output value											
a. Initial planned value	Y 10,000	250.00	1,200.00	1,320.00	2,000.00	2,350.00	1,890.00	1,800.00	1,800.00	1,300.00	1,340.00
Date initial plan promulgated	month	Oct 1964	Oct 1972	Oct 1974	Oct 1975	Oct 1976	Oct 1977	Oct 1978	Oct 1979	Oct 1980	Oct 1981
b. Number of revisions of annual plan											
c. Final planned value	Y 10,000	250.00	1,200.00	1,320.00	2,000.00	2,350.00	1,890.00	1,800.00	1,800.00	1,300.00	1,340.00
Exact date final plan determined	month	Jul 1965	Jul 1973	Jul 1975	Jul 1976	Jul 1977	Jul 1978	Jul 1979	Jul 1980	Jul 1981	Jul 1982
29. Annual total profits											
a. Initial planned value	Y 10,000	25.00	210.00	200.00	n.a.*	250.00	300.00	250.00	250.00	140.00	110.00
Date initial plan promulgated	month	Jan 1965	Feb 1973	Feb 1975	-	Feb 1977	Feb 1978	-	-	Feb 1981	Feb 1982
b. Number of revisions of annual plan	time	-	-	-	-	-	1	-	-	1	-
c. Final planned value	Y 10,000	-	-	-	-	-	340.00	-	-	70.00	-
Exact date final plan determined	month	-	-	-	-	-	Aug 1978	-	-	Oct 1981	-
30. Profits handed over to higher levels											
a. Initial planned value	Y 10,000										
Date initial plan promulgated	month										
b. Number of revisions of annual plan											
c. Final planned value	Y 10,000										
Exact date final plan determined	month										

* Not promulgated.

Item	Units	1965	1973	1975	1976	1977	1978	1979	1980	1981	1982
VIII. Input Consumption											
31. Ratios of material input consumption to output produced of major commodities											
a. J53-160B press	ton/Y 10,000	4.57	-	4.57	4.57	5.39	5.39	5.39	5.39	5.39	5.03
b. J53-300 press	"	3.45	3.45	3.45	3.45	4.56	4.56	4.56	4.56	4.56	4.28
c. J53-400 press	"	-	1.41	1.41	1.41	1.23	1.23	1.23	1.23	1.23	1.09
d. J53-630 press	"	-	0.57	0.57	0.57	0.43	0.43	0.43	0.43	0.43	0.40
32. Energy consumption											
Total consumption of electricity during year	10,000 kWh	-	301.52	318.00	296.80	346.79	311.00	284.00	320.00	292.20	302.00
Of which: Power consumed in industrial production	"	41.17	238.84	252.79	291.94	339.93	304.50	277.56	314.02	278.80	289.59
Total consumption of coal during year	ton	894.00	3,472.00	3,433.00	2,760.00	2,800.00	2,186.60	2,968.04	2,153.69	3,764.44	4,765.84
Total consumption of fuel oil during year	ton	16.36	-	-	-	-	1,829.27	822.96	430.57	147.39	131.84
33. Amount of electricity consumed per unit of output of major products	kwh per Y 10,000 of output value	1,249	1,989	1,479	1,280	1,321	1,611	1,316	1,504	1,684	1,668
34. Amount of coal consumed per unit of output of major products	tons per Y 10,000 of output value	2.71	2.89	2.01	1.21	1.09	1.16	1.41	1.03	2.27	2.98

Item	Units	1965	1973	1975	1976	1977	1978	1979	1980	1981	1982
35. Amount of fuel oil consumed per unit of output of major products	tons per Y 10,000 of output value	0.05	-	-	-	-	0.97	0.39	0.21	0.09	0.08
IX. Inventories											
36. Year-end inventories of major outputs											
a. J53-160B press	set	-	-	-	-	-	-	-	4	13	-
b. J53-300 press	"	-	-	-	5	3	2	-	3	-	14
c. J53-400 press	"	-	-	-	-	24	19	5	4	1	-
d. J53-630 press	"	-	-	-	-	1	1	-	6	-	3
37. Year-end inventories of major inputs											
a. Coal	ton	-	-	-	-	-	-	-	-	-	132.80
b Coke	"	-	-	-	-	-	-	-	-	-	43.00
c. Fuel oil	"	-	-	-	-	-	-	-	-	-	11.90
d. Steel	"	-	-	-	-	-	-	-	-	-	99.40
e. Others											
- cast iron	"	-	-	-	-	-	-	-	-	-	182.90
- cast copper	"	-	-	-	-	-	-	-	-	-	35.00

Item	Units	1965	1973	1975	1976	1977	1978	1979	1980	1981	1982
38. Amount of fuel oil consumed per unit of output of major products											
a. J53-160B press	set	-	-	1	-	-	5	2	-	-	2
b. J53-300 press	"	-	8	1	4	4	5	-	-	-	1
c. J53-400 press	"	-	-	13	6	10	10	-	-	1	3
d. J53-630 press	"	-	-	1	-	-	-	-	1	-	1

World Bank Publications of Related Interest

A Brief Review of the World Lube Oils Industry

A. Ceyhan, H. Kohli, L. Wijetilleke, and B.R. Choudhury

This report assesses the structure, background, and outlook for the world lube oils industry. Presents the historical and projected lube oils demand and trends in manufacturing technologies and production capacity and provides an indicative assessment of the economics of lube oil production with detailed market and economic data.

Energy Industries Report Series No. 1. 1982. 48 pages (including 13 annexes, references).

ISBN 0-8213-0054-7. Stock No. BK 0054. $3.

Capital Utilization in Manufacturing: Colombia, Israel, Malaysia, and the Philippines

Romeo M. Bautista, Helen Hughes, David Lim, David Morawetz, and Francisco E. Thoumi

The authors surveyed 1,200 manufacturing firms in four developing countries to establish actual levels of capital utilization. The information collected was the first and remains the only data base available for the study of capital utilization. It was found that capital utilization is not as low as had been supposed. The study is concerned with factors that cause differences in levels of capital utilization and the policies that might be used to increase it.

Oxford University Press, 1982. 288 pages (including bibliography, index).

LC 81-9526. ISBN 0-19-520268-6, Stock No. OX 520268. $22 hardcover.

The Construction Industry: Issues and Strategies in Developing Countries

Ernesto E. Henriod, coordinating author

Presents a profile of the construction industry. Points out that construction work represents 3 to 8 percent of the gross domestic product of developing countries. Fostering a domestic capability in construction, therefore, is important. Discusses problems and constraints of the industry and formulates strategies for future actions. Draws heavily from the experience of the World Bank in supporting domestic construction industries over the past ten years. Useful to contractors, engineers, and administrators in construction industry.

1984. 120 pages.

ISBN 0-8213-0268-X. Stock No. BK 0268. $5.

Cost-Benefit Evaluation of LDC Industrial Sectors Which Have Foreign Ownership

Garry G. Pursell

Staff Working Paper No. 465. 1981. 45 pages.

Stock No. WP 0465. $3.

Development Finance Companies

Examines the role of development finance companies as major mechanisms for assisting medium-scale productive industries, assesses their potential for aiding small enterprises in meeting socioeconomic objectives of developing countries, and discusses the evolution of World Bank assistance to them.

Sector Policy Paper. 1976. 68 pages (including 7 annexes).

Stock Nos. BK 9040 (English), BK 9058 (French), BK 9041 (Spanish). $5.

Empirical Justification for Infant Industry Protection

Larry E. Westphal

Staff Working Paper No. 445. 1981. 38 pages (including references).

Stock No. WP 0445. $3.

Employment and Development of Small Enterprises

David L. Gordon, coordinating author

Examines the potential role of the World Bank in encouraging developing countries to assist small enterprises and suggests that efficient substitution of labor for capital is possible in a broad spectrum of small-scale manufacturing and other activities that are able to absorb a rapidly growing labor force.

Sector Policy Paper. 1978. 93 pages (including 3 annexes).

Stock Nos. BK 9060 (English), BK 9061 (French), BK 9062 (Spanish). $5.

Estimating Total Factor Productivity Growth in a Developing Country

Anne O. Krueger and Baran Tuncer

Staff Working Paper No. 422. 1980. 64 pages (including references, appendix).

Stock No. WP 0422. $3.

Financing Small-Scale Industry and Agriculture in Developing Countries: The Merits and Limitations of "Commercial" Policies

Dennis Anderson and Farida Khambata

Staff Working Paper No. 519. 1982. 41 pages (including references).

ISBN-0-8213-0007-5. Stock No. WP 0519. $3.

Fostering the Capital-Goods Sector in LDCs: A Survey of Evidence and Requirements

Howard Pack

Staff Working Paper No. 376. 1980. 64 pages (including references).

Stock No. WP 0376. $3.

Incorporating Uncertainty into Planning of Industrialization Strategies for Developing Countries

Alexander H. Sarris and Irma Adelman

Staff Working Paper No. 503. 1982. 58 pages (including appendix, references).

Stock No. WP-0503. $3.

Industrialization and Growth: The Experience of Large Countries
Hollis Chenery

Staff Working Paper No. 539. 1982. 38 pages.

ISBN 0-8213-0097-0. Stock No. WP 0539. $3.

Industrial Prospects and Policies in the Developed Countries
Bela Balassa

Staff Working Paper No. 453. 1981. 30 pages (including appendix).

Stock No. WP 0453. $3.

Industrial Strategy for Late Starters: The Experience of Kenya, Tanzania and Zambia
Ravi Gulhati and Uday Sekhar

Staff Working Paper No. 457. 1981. 63 pages (including references, annex).

Stock No. WP 0457. $3.

Korean Industrial Competence: Where It Came From
Larry E. Westphal, Yung W. Rhee, and Garry G. Pursell

Staff Working Paper No. 469. 1981. 76 pages (including references).

Stock No. WP 0469. $3.

NEW

Location Factors in the Decentralization of Industry: A Survey of Metropolitan Sao Paulo, Brazil
Peter M. Townroe

Focuses on decisionmaking procedures for industrial companies that are establishing new plants or relocating their plant sites. Some 581 industrial companies in Brazil participated in a 1980 survey to determine company motives for seeking a new site or building. Appendixes include nine detailed tables useful to industrial planners and company plant developers.

Staff Working Paper No. 517. 1983. 112 pages.

ISBN 0-8213-0005-9. Stock No. WP 0517. $5.

Macroeconomic Implications of Factor Substitution in Industrial Processes
Howard Pack

Staff Working Paper No. 377. 1980. 67 pages (including bibliography).

Stock No. WP 0377. $3.

Made in Jamaica: The Development of the Manufacturing Sector
Mahmood Ali Ayub

This book, the first detailed study of Jamaica's manufacturing sector, provides a comprehensive assessment of the important characteristics of the sector and of its structure. It relates the development of the sector during the past two decades, describes the extent of protection provided to the sector in 1978, and examines the prospects for growth of manufactured exports during the coming years. Policy recommendations are made on the basis of this analysis.

The Johns Hopkins University Press, 1981. 144 pages.

LC 80-27765. ISBN 0-8018-2568-7, Stock No. JH 2568, $6.50 paperback.

Managerial Structures and Practices in Manufacturing Enterprises: A Yugoslav Case Study
Martin Schrenk

Staff Working Paper No. 455. 1981. 104 pages (including 4 appendixes).

Stock No. WP 0455. $5.

Managing State-Owned Enterprises
Mary M. Shirley

Discusses efficiency of state-owned enterprises. Gives the nature and size of this sector, including industrial and commercial firms, mines, utilities, transport companies, and financial intermediaries controlled to some extent by government. Tells how to increase the sector's efficiency by defining objectives, controlling without interference, holding managers accountable for results, and designing managerial skills and incentives. Includes bar graphs and charts of information for 24 developing and developed countries.

Staff Working Paper No. 577. 1983. 116 pages.

ISBN 0-8213-0241-8. Stock No. WP 0577. $5.

Manufacture of Heavy Electrical Equipment in Developing Countries
Ayhan Çilingiroğlu

Analyzes growth and competitiveness, comparing prices and costs with those in the international market.

The Johns Hopkins University Press, 1969. 235 pages (including 2 annexes).

LC 76-89962. ISBN 0-8018-1097-3, $5.50 paperback.

Spanish: Fabricación de equipo eléctrico pesado en los países en desarrollo. Editorial Tecnos, 1971. $5.50 paperback.

The Mining Industry and the Developing Countries
Rex Bosson and Bension Varon

An overview of the world's nonfuel mining industry, its structure and operation, and the major factors bearing on them.

Oxford University Press, 1977; 3rd printing, 1984. 304 pages (including 12 appendixes, bibliography, index).

LC 77-2983. ISBN 0-19-920096-3, Stock No. OX 920096, $29.50 hardcover; ISBN 0-19-920099-8, Stock No. OX 920099, $14.95 paperback.

French: L'industrie miniere dans le tiers monde. Economica, 1978. ISBN 2-7178-0030-1, Stock No. IB 0538, $14.95.

Spanish: La industria minera y los paises en desarrollo. Editorial Tecnos, 1978. ISBN 84-309-0779-3, Stock No. IB 0521, $14.95.

Occupational Structures of Industries

Manuel Zymelman

Eighty-four tables profile the occupational composition of industries in each of twenty-six countries. Data show the structure of employment by sectors and industries for each country; cross-classify 120 occupations with fifty-eight industries; and provide information about productivity (value added per person engaged), energy consumption per person engaged, and employment.

1980; second printing, 1982. 211 pages.

ISBN 0-8213-0126-8. Stock No. BK 0126. $20.

Policies for Industrial Progress in Developing Countries

John Cody, Helen Hughes, and David Wall, editors

Analysis of the principal policy issues that influence the course and pace of industrialization in the developing countries. The text, organized along lines of governmental administrative responsibility for various industrial policies, includes chapters on trade, finance, labor-technology relations, taxation, licensing and other direct production controls, public enterprises, infrastructure and location, industry-agriculture linkage, and the international environment.

Oxford University Press, 1980; 2nd printing, 1982. 325 pages (including bibliography, index).

LC 79-24786. ISBN 0-19-520176-0, Stock No. OX 520176, $24.95 hardcover; ISBN 0-19-520177-9, Stock No. OX 520177, $9.95 paperback.

The Planning of Investment Programs

Alexander Meeraus and Ardy J. Stoutjesdijk, editors

Series comprising three volumes (to date) that describe a systematic approach to investment planning, relying primarily on mathematical programming techniques. Includes both general methodological volumes and studies dealing with specific industrial subsectors.

Volume 1: The Planning of Industrial Investment Programs: A Methodology

David A. Kendrick and Ardy J. Stoutjesdijk

The analytical approach with special emphasis on the complications arising from economies of scale; a helpful introduction to linear and mixed-integer programming, facilitating understanding of subsequent volumes in the series.

The Johns Hopkins University Press, 1979. 144 pages (including index).

LC 78-8428. ISBN 0-8018-2139-8, Stock No. JH 2139, $18.50 hardcover; ISBN 0-8018-2152-5, Stock No. JH 2152, $12 paperback.

French: La programmation des investissements industriels: methode et etude de cas. Economica, 1981. (Combines translation of this book with that of the case study of the fertilizer industry in Volume 2, below.) ISBN 2-7178-0328-9, Stock No. IB 0544, $12.

Volume 2: The Planning of Investment Programs in the Fertilizer Industry

Armeane M. Choksi, Alexander Meeraus, and Ardy J. Stoutjesdijk

Discusses the main products and processes of relevance to fertilizer production and a systematic description of the planning problems that need to be addressed during the project identification phase.

The Johns Hopkins University Press, 1980. 320 pages.

LC 78-8436. ISBN 0-8018-2138-X, Stock No. JH 2138, $25 hardcover; ISBN 0-8018-2153-3, Stock No. JH 2153, $15 paperback.

NEW

Volume 3: The Planning of Investment Programs in the Steel Industry

David A. Kendrick, Alexander Meeraus, and Jaime Alatorre

As a supplier of both capital equipment and materials for further processing, the steel industry has a substantial effect on the cost structure and competitiveness of other economic activities. Its own cost structure, however, depends to a large extent on the efficiency of past investments.

Provides an overview of the technology of steel production, and the problems of investment analysis in this industry, and contains an application of investment analysis to the Mexican steel industry. Introduces a new economic modeling language, GAMS, which decreases the time and effort required to construct and use industrial sector models.

The Johns Hopkins University Press. 1984. 328 pages.

LC 83-18722. ISBN 0-8018-3197-0, Stock No. JH 3197, $30 hardcover; ISBN 0-8018-3198-9, Stock No. JH 3198, $15 paperback.

Pollution Control in Sao Paulo, Brazil: Costs, Benefits, and Effects on Industrial Location

Vinod Thomas

Staff Working Paper No. 501. 1981. 127 pages (including annex, references).

Stock No. WP 0501. $5.

The Process of Industrial Development and Alternative Development Strategies

Bela Balassa

Staff Working Paper No. 438. 1980. 42 pages (including appendix).

Stock No. WP 0438. $3.

Public Subsidies to Industry: The Case of Sweden and Its Shipbuilding Industry

Carl Hamilton

Examines the reasons for the high government subsidies given to the Swedish shipbuilding industry during the recession period of the 1970s. Sweden's approach to the shipbuilding problem is compared with the adjustment made by Japan when it faced a similar situation. Concludes that a stabilization policy is important in achieving the objective of full employment.

Staff Working Paper No. 566. 1983. 52 pages.

ISBN 0-8213-0196-9. Stock no. WP 0566. $3.

Restructuring of Manufacturing Industry: The Experience of the Textile Industry in Pakistan, Philippines, Portugal, and Turkey

Barend A. de Vries and Willem Brakel

Views the restructuring and modernization of manufacturing from the perspective of World Bank assistance in the textile industry. Evaluates the roles of government, the financial system and the private sector in restructuring.

World Bank Working paper No. 558. 1983. 59 pages.

ISBN 0-8213-0151-9. Stock No. WP 0558. $3.

Small Enterprises and Development Policy in the Philippines: A Case Study
Dennis Anderson and Farida Khambata

Staff Working Paper No. 468. 1981. 239 pages (including bibliography, annex).

Stock No. WP 0468. $10.

Small Industry in Developing Countries: Some Issues
Dennis Anderson

Staff Working Paper No. 518. 1982. 77 pages (including references).

ISBN 0-8213-0006-7. Stock No. WP 0518. $3.

Small-Scale Enterprises in Korea and Taiwan
Sam P.S. Ho

Staff Working Paper No. 384. 1980. 157 pages (including 4 appendixes).

Stock No. WP 0384. $5.

NEW

Sources of Industrial Growth and Structural Change: The Case of Turkey
Merih Celasun

Considers the role of Turkey's public and private sectors in the industrial transition since the 1950s. Compares Turkey's trade prospects in the 1980s with growth in earlier periods of development as well as growth in other semi-industrial countries.

Staff Working Paper No. 614. 1983. 188 pages.

ISBN 0-8213-0283-2. Stock No. WP 0614. $5.

State Manufacturing Enterprise in a Mixed Economy: The Turkish Case
Bertil Wålstedt

Traces the historic roots of "etatism" and reviews the performance of six major state industries in Turkey.

The Johns Hopkins University Press, 1980. 354 pages (including appendixes, index).

LC 78-21398. ISBN 0-8018-2226-2, Stock No. JH 2226, $30 hardcover; ISBN 0-8018-2227-0, Stock No. JH 2227, $13.50 paperback.

NEW

Technological Change and Industrial Development: Issues and Opportunities
Frederick T. Moore

Identifies principal issues relating technological change to growth in industrial development. Draws upon the theoretical and empirical literature for an economic analysis of effective program designs. Projects underway in the engineering and capital goods industries suggests methods for revising policies and promoting new technological information in industry.

Staff Working Paper No. 613. 1983. 96 pages.

ISBN 0-8213-0257-4. Stock No. WP 0613. $3.

Transition toward More Rapid and Labor-Intensive Industrial Development: The Case of the Philippines
Barend A. de Vries

Staff Working Paper No. 424. 1980. 32 pages (including references, 12 tables).

Stock No. WP 0424. $3.

Prices subject to change without notice and may vary by country.

The World Bank Publications Order Form

SEND TO: **YOUR LOCAL DISTRIBUTOR** OR TO **WORLD BANK PUBLICATIONS**
(See the other side of this form.)
P.O. BOX 37525
WASHINGTON, D.C. 20013 U.S.A.

Date ____________

Name ____________

Title ____________

Firm ____________

Address ____________

City ________ State ____ Postal Code ________

Country ________ Telephone (____) ________

Purchaser Reference No. ____________

Ship to: (Enter if different from purchaser)

Name ____________

Title ____________

Firm ____________

Address ____________

City ________ State ____ Postal Code ________

Country ________ Telephone (____) ________

Check your method of payment.
Enclosed is my ☐ Check ☐ International Money Order ☐ Unesco Coupons ☐ International Postal Coupon.
Make payable to World Bank Publications for U.S. dollars unless you are ordering from your local distributor.

Charge my ☐ VISA ☐ MasterCard ☐ American Express ☐ Choice. (Credit cards accepted only for orders addressed to World Bank Publications.)

Credit Card Account Number ____________ Expiration Date ____________ Signature ____________

☐ Invoice me and please reference my Purchase Order No. ____________.

Please ship me the items listed below.

Stock Number	Author/ Title	Customer Internal Routing Code	Quantity	Unit Price	Total Amount $

All prices subject to change. Prices may vary by country. Allow 6–8 weeks for delivery.

Subtotal Cost $______

Total copies ______ Air mail surcharge if desired ($2.00 each) $______

Postage and handling for more than two complimentary items ($2.00 each) $______

Total $______

Thank you for your order.

IBRD-0053

Distributors of World Bank Publications

ARGENTINA
Carlos Hirsch, SRL,
Attn: Ms. Monica Bustos
Florida 165 4° piso
Galeria Guemes
Buenos Aires 1307

AUSTRALIA, PAPUA NEW GUINEA, FIJI, SOLOMON ISLANDS, WESTERN SAMOA, AND VANUATU
The Australian Financial Review
Information Service (AFRIS)
Attn: Mr. David Jamieson
235-243 Jones Street
Broadway
Sydney, NSW 20001

BELGIUM
Publications des Nations Unies
Attn: Mr. Jean de Lannoy
av. du Roi 202
1060 Brussels

CANADA
Le Diffuseur
Attn: Mrs. Suzanne Vermette
C.P. 85, Boucherville J4B 5E6
Quebec

COSTA RICA
Libreria Trejos
Attn: Mr. Hugo Chamberlain
Calle 11-13, Av. Fernandez Guell
San Jose

DENMARK
Sanfundslitteratur
Attn: Mr. Wilfried Roloff
Rosenderns Alle 11
DK-1970 Copenhagen V.

EGYPT, Arab Republic of
Al Ahram
Al Galaa Street
Cairo

FINLAND
Akateeminen Kirjakauppa
Attn: Mr. Kari Litmanen
Keskuskatu 1, SF-00100
Helsinki 10

FRANCE
World Bank Publications
66, avenue d'Iéna
75116 Paris

GERMANY, Federal Republic of
UNO-Verlag
Attn: Mr. Joachim Krause
Simrockstrasse 23
D-5300 Bonn 1

HONG KONG, MACAU
Asia 2000 Ltd.
Attn: Ms. Gretchen Wearing Smith
6 Fl., 146 Prince Edward Road
Kowloon

INDIA
UBS Publishers' Distributors Ltd.
Attn: Mr. D.P. Veer
5 Ansari Road, Post Box 7015
New Delhi 110002
(Branch offices in Bombay, Bangalore, Kanpur, Calcutta, and Madras)

INDONESIA
Pt. Indira Limited
Attn: Mr. Bambang Wahyudi
Jl, Dr. Sam Ratulangi No. 37
Jakarta Pusat

IRELAND
TDC Publishers
Attn: Mr. James Booth
12 North Frederick Street
Dublin 1

ITALY
Licosa Commissionaria Sansoni SPA
Attn: Mr. Giancarlo Bigazzi
Via Lamarmora 45
50121
Florence

JAPAN
Eastern Book Service
Attn: Mr. Terumasa Hirano
37-3, Hongo 3-Chome, Bunkyo-ku 113
Tokyo

KENYA
Africa Book Services (E.A.) Ltd.
Attn: Mr. M.B. Dar
P.O. Box 45245
Nairobi

KOREA, REPUBLIC OF
Pan Korea Book Corporation
Attn: Mr. Yoon-Sun Kim
P.O. Box 101, Kwanghwamun
Seoul

MALAYSIA
University of Malaya Cooperative Bookshop Ltd.
Attn: Mr. Mohammed Fahim Htj Yacob
P.O. Box 1127, Jalan Pantai Baru
Kuala Lumpur

MEXICO
INFOTEC
Attn: Mr. Jorge Cepeda
San Lorenzo 153-11, Col. del Valle,
Deleg. Benito Juarez
03100 Mexico, D.F.

MIDDLE EAST
Middle East Marketing Research Bureau
Attn: Mr. George Vassilou
Mitsis Bldg. 3
Makarios III Avenue
Nicosia
Cyprus
(Branch offices in Bahrain, Greece, Morocco, Kuwait, United Arab Emirates, Jordan)

NETHERLANDS
MBE BV
Attn: Mr. Gerhard van Bussell
Noorderwal 38,
7241 BL Lochem

NORWAY
Johan Grundt Tanum A.S.
Attn: Ms. Randi Mikkelborg
P.O. Box 1177 Sentrum
Oslo 1

PANAMA
Ediciones Libreria Cultural Panamena
Attn: Mr. Luis Fernandez Fraguela R.
Av. 7, Espana 16
Panama Zone 1

PHILIPPINES
National Book Store
Attn: Mrs. Socorro C. Ramos
701 Rizal Avenue
Manila

PORTUGAL
Livraria Portugal
Attn: Mr. Antonio Alves Martins
Rua Do Carmo 70-74
1200
Lisbon

SAUDI ARABIA
Jarir Book Store
Attn: Mr. Akram Al-Agil
P.O. Box 3196
Riyadh

SINGAPORE, TAIWAN, BURMA
Information Publications Private, Ltd.
Attn: Ms. Janet David
02-06 1st Floor, Pei-Fu Industrial Building
24 New Industrial Road
Singapore

SPAIN
Mundi-Prensa Libros, S.A.
Attn: Mr. J.M. Hernandez
Castello 37
Madrid

SRI LANKA AND THE MALDIVES
Lake House Bookshop
Attn: Mr. Victor Walatara
41 Wad Ramanayake Mawatha
Colombo 2

SWEDEN
ABCE Fritzes Kungl, Hovbokhandel
Attn: Mr. Eide Segerback
Regeringsgatan 12, Box 16356
S-103 27 Stockholm

SWITZERLAND
Librairie Payot
Attn: Mr. Henri de Perrot
6, rue Grenus
1211 Geneva

TANZANIA
Oxford University Press
Attn: Mr. Anthony Theobold
Maktaba Road, P.O. Box 5299
Dar es Salaam

THAILAND
Central Department Store, Head Office
Attn: Mrs. Ratana
306 Silom Road
Bangkok

Thailand Management Association
Attn: Mrs. Sunan
308 Silom Road
Bangkok

TUNISIA
Société Tunisienne de Diffusion
Attn: Mr. Slaheddine Ben Hamida
5 Avenue de Carthage
Tunis

TURKEY
Haset Kitapevi A.S.
Attn: Mr. Izzet Izerel
469, Istiklal Caddesi
Beyoglu-Istanbul

UNITED KINGDOM AND NORTHERN IRELAND
Microinfo Ltd.
Attn: Mr. Roy Selwyn
Newman Lane, P.O. Box 3
Alton, Hampshire GU34 2PG
England

UNITED STATES
The World Bank Book Store
600 19th Street, N.W.
Washington, D.C. 20433
(Postal address: P.O. Box 37525
Washington, D.C. 20013, U.S.A.)

Baker and Taylor Company
501 South Gladiola Avenue
Momence, Illinois, 60954

380 Edison Way
Reno, Nevada, 89564

50 Kirby Avenue
Somerville, New Jersey, 08876

Commerce, Georgia 30599

Bernan Associates
9730-E George Palmer Highway
Lanham, Maryland, 20761

Blackwell North America, Inc.
1001 Fries Mill Road
Blackwood, New Jersey 08012

Sidney Kramer Books
1722 H Street, N.W.
Washington, D.C. 20006

United Nations Bookshop
United Nations Plaza
New York, N.Y. 10017

VENEZUELA
Libreria del Este
Attn. Mr. Juan Pericas
Avda Francisco de Miranda, no. 52
Edificio Galipan, Aptdo. 60.337
Caracas 1060-A